The New News

v.

The Old News

PERSPECTIVES
ON THE NEWS

The NEW NEWS

v.

The Old News

The Press *and* Politics in the 1990s

Essays by

Jay Rosen ✦ Paul Taylor

Series Editor: Suzanne Charlé

A Twentieth Century Fund Paper

The Twentieth Century Fund is a research foundation undertaking timely analyses of economic, political, and social issues. Not-for-profit and nonpartisan, the Fund was founded in 1919 and endowed by Edward A. Filene.

Library of Congress Cataloging-in-Publication Data

Rosen, Jay, 1956–
    The new news v. the old news : press and politics in the 1990s / essays by Jay Rosen and Paul Taylor
        p.   cm. — (Perspectives on the news series)
    Includes bibliographical references and index.
    ISBN 0-87078-344-0 : $9.95
        1. Press and politics—United States—History—20th century.
2. American newspapers—History—20th century. 3. Television broadcasting of news—United States. 4. United States—Politics and government—20th century. I. Taylor, Paul, 1949– . II. Title. III. Title: New News versus the old news. IV. Series.
PN4888.P6R67 1992
302.23'0973'09049—dc20   92-32299
                                                                                    CIP

Cover Design: Claude Goodwin
Manufactured in the United States of America.
Copyright © 1992 by the Twentieth Century Fund, Inc.

Foreword

Communication between voters and their political leaders is central to the functioning of a democracy. No authoritarian system can long survive a people fully informed, nor can a democracy thrive when voters do not understand the consequences of their actions. As a result of these truths, there is intense concern about the way our media communicate the ideas of our leaders and potential leaders to the people.

This concern is no mere intellectual exercise. In modern politics, the media provide the intervening lens that selects most of the campaign experience the American voters—and nonvoters—actually have. In fact, the very essence of democratic education and practice in this country is part of a larger ocean of news, information, and entertainment. This increasingly complex and omnipresent world of television, radio, newspapers, and magazines is responsible for much of what shapes our perceptions about the nation and the world. The problem is that participants in politics, including reporters, often confuse the experience that *they* are having with that of the public.

Whatever the outcome of the 1992 election, the early media coverage of the campaign justifiably provoked reactions that varied from disappointment to nothing short of outrage. The emphasis on gossip, scandal, trivia—what's called "tabloid journalism"—was decried by citizens, politicians, scholars, and media representatives themselves.

A host of reasons, many of substance, have been offered for the carnival atmosphere and sensational news focus. One obvious explanation, of course, is an old one: this stuff sells. In this sense, the coverage of campaigns may well be getting closer to a pure market outcome for the news *business*, which may not be surprising given how rapidly the "media" are changing in terms of ownership, technology, purpose, and format. (Perhaps the really amazing thing is that there has been so *much* restraint in past political coverage.) Whatever the causes, a variety of reform ideas, some old, a few novel, are being offered as possible remedies for the "problem."

In response to these developments and concerns, the Twentieth Century Fund in 1991 decided to initiate a series of studies exploring the state of modern media. The essays that follow were written during the summer of 1992. While they are grounded, to some extent, in a long period of development and change in American media, they also are very much a product of the unique circumstances of these times.

Thus, given the Fund's focus on public policy and governance, these essays are a particularly appropriate first volume for our series, Perspectives on the News. The series eventually will include monographs on the future of newspapers, the development of global television news services, privacy and libel litigation and its effects on a free press, and "virtual reality" and the news. In addition to this series, the Fund has a number of media-related projects under way, including studies of the technology and public policy implications of the "global information economy," research on concentration of media ownership, and two Fund Task Forces—one on the future of public television in the United States and the other on television coverage of the 1992 presidential campaign.

In this volume's first essay, Jay Rosen, associate professor of journalism at New York University, takes on the question of press responsibility and professionalism at the most fundamental level. He argues for a new "public agenda for journalism"—one that accepts and reacts to the fact of the profession's central role in the practice of democracy. While we understand that, to be truly free, a press must be unencumbered by public rules and regulations, we surely do not mean that an unexamined press is worth having. Moreover, the very professionalism so treasured by members of the fourth estate must stand for more than simply what sells. At minimum, we can hope for an increase in peer pressure among journalists: more shame and guilt for the bad actors, and alternatively more approval and applause for those who cover the campaign responsibly.

Paul Taylor, an exceptional journalist in his own right, confronts the practical possibilities of dramatically changing nothing less than the terms of presidential campaign engagement, and thus the nature of campaign focus and coverage. He explores the implications of "infotainment" and the "new news," and discusses standards by which journalists should conduct themselves. He also returns to one of the few reform proposals that might actually improve the quality of debate and lower the cost of campaigns—free air time for presidential candidates—and provides an eloquent argument in its favor.

The question for this and future election years is, what can be done to influence the mix of coverage we are getting? Is there, for example, any role for good taste? Can we restore gossip to its proper, lowly place among the considerations that go into choosing a president? Are we capable of insisting that campaign coverage emphasize issues and values? These are among the issues explored in this volume, and in papers by Kathleen Hall Jamieson, Ken Auletta, and Thomas Patterson that will be published later this year.

The Fund's current work in this field builds on a long tradition. Since the early 1970s, we have been interested in the media—both print and electronic—and particularly its coverage of and effects on the American electorate. Our reports have examined such diverse issues as the effects of television on presidential elections (*Presidential Television* by Newton Minow, Lee Mitchell, and John Bartlow Martin), the problems of coverage of international events (*The International News Services* by Jonathan Fenby), the relationship between government and the press (*Press Freedoms Under Pressure: Report of the Task Force on the Government and the Press; A Free and Responsive Press: The Report of the Task Force for a National News Council*), and the issue of televised presidential debates (*Beyond Debate, For Great Debates,* and *A Proper Institution*).

Political campaigns in the late 1980s and 1990s have raised a host of new challenges for the media. The essays in this volume go beyond explaining those challenges, to propose how the media can think and act to surmount them. We thank the authors for their efforts. For we believe that democracy thrives in an atmosphere of open debate and criticism. On the whole, the Great Republic coexists quite nicely with selfishness, greed, and the drive for votes on the one hand and market share on the other. But we have the right and perhaps the obligation to demand more from our press. We certainly do from our presidents, insisting that they reflect a great many of our values beyond mere commitment to the free enterprise system. Can a press driven largely by the marketplace adequately report and judge the candidates for chief executive and the deeper values they represent? In 1992, that is a tough question. Democracy may indeed give us the leadership we deserve. But when it comes to the media, it may not be enough to get only what we pay for.

Richard C. Leone, *President*
The Twentieth Century Fund
September 1992

Contents

Foreword   by Richard C. Leone   v

1. **Politics, Vision, and the Press: Toward a Public Agenda
    for Journalism**   by Jay Rosen   3

2. **Political Coverage in the 1990s: Teaching the Old News
    New Tricks**   by Paul Taylor   37

Index   71

About the Authors   75

Politics, Vision, and the Press:
Toward a Public Agenda for Journalism

by Jay Rosen

B eginning in 1988, journalists repeatedly reminded us of George Bush's clumsy reference to the "vision thing." For four years, they produced news articles, television reports, and editorial columns on the president's alleged difficulties in articulating a philosophy for his administration, and a long-term agenda for the country. It is curious that throughout this time, no one, including the president's defenders, sought to turn the question around. What sort of philosophy have journalists articulated about their own role in a troubled democracy? What sort of vision do they exhibit as they go about the business of reporting and commenting on public life? What is the long-term agenda of the press, or does it have its eye only on the immediate flare-ups and minor controversies that make for good headlines but matter little to the nation's future?

We are accustomed to silence on such questions. Journalists are generally not expected to declare their philosophical outlook or political intentions. Indeed, we would be shocked and frightened if, say, the editor of the *New York Times* began talking about the direction in which he wanted to take the country. But this does not mean that journalism couldn't use more self-direction, a firmer grounding, an articulate philosophy that envisions a better future and asks journalists to help achieve it. These may be difficult matters to discuss, but they are surely not beyond discussion—particularly at a time when American politics, by journalists' own accounts, is in a severe state of disrepair.[1]

Members of the news media have gained a good deal of influence and prominent standing in politics during the past thirty years. But with few exceptions the "vision thing" has eluded them. It may be time, then, to turn the question around: What is the proper agenda of the American press? What should it be trying to achieve as an influential force in our political culture? What principles can guide the construction of its agenda? By struggling with these questions, the press might point itself toward a new public philosophy, toward an improved method of explaining its place in politics and its role in public life. With these improvements, the press might also begin to speak with more authority and fortify its considerable—though, in some ways, waning—influence in the American public sphere.

To speak of "the press" is to refer to an occupational group—those who, in any medium, report on politics and public life with some intention of making sense out it. Whether this group constitutes a profession is often disputed; but there is no disputing the common culture and occupational mindset that includes journalists at both the *Wall Street Journal* and *USA Today*, "The MacNeil/Lehrer Newshour" and CNN, the *Boston Globe* and the *Fresno Bee*, ABC News and "Fox Five." It is the shared culture of the newsroom that makes it possible to speak of "the press," although this term does not refer to something as well organized and distinct as, say, the military.

Media critic Jon Katz has recently argued that the Old News provided by the press is being eclipsed in popularity (and relevance) by the New News, which comes via Jay Leno, Hollywood, MTV, and rap music.[2] In the companion paper in this volume, Paul Taylor discusses in some depth the rise of the New News and its effect on the Old News. In addressing myself to the Old News and its practitioners, I do not mean to ignore the rise of the new, but to suggest that the old may need to rethink its purpose in a world of shifting allegiances.

"The press" is admittedly an antiquated term, but one we should try to preserve for the simple reason that it resonates with the language of the republic. That is why we continue to speak of freedom of the press, but not freedom of the media; we give people press passes, but not media passes. "The press," in short, is the republic's name for what the society increasingly calls "the media." To discuss the press and its prospects is thus to concern oneself with the fortunes of the republic, to insist that a consumer society also be seen as a political community. Journalism, properly grounded, insists on the priority of political life, and this is one reason that it must be strengthened and improved.

The 1988 presidential campaign, widely denounced as one of the worst in modern memory, led many journalists to the conclusion that something was wrong in the reporting of politics. A good number thought that it was the press, and not only the candidates, who had failed the country.[3] Disgust with the campaign brought with it an unusual number of conferences, panel discussions, and in-house critiques.[4] But despite all the talk the changes in 1992 have been marginal rather than fundamental: more televised debates, less attention to photo opportunities, deemphasizing the ritual of the campaign plane, an effort to focus on voters instead of handlers, some sharper criticisms of campaign ads, some better background pieces on the candidates. These are welcome adjustments, but they do not reflect a radically new approach to campaign coverage.

At the time this paper was completed (mid-August), what stood out from the events of 1992 wasn't the courage and enterprise of the press, but two other developments that have given journalists and critics considerable pause. One is the spectacular return of what political scientist Larry Sabato calls the "feeding frenzy" mentality in the press, especially evident in the reporting of Gennifer Flowers's allegations and the so-called character issues that almost consumed Bill Clinton in the early stages of his campaign.[5] The other outstanding development is the sudden political prominence of the new media, particularly call-in shows like "Donahue" and "Larry King Live," where voters rather than journalists pose the questions.[6] If the first development shows the inability of the press to control its most predictable excesses, the second signals the growing irrelevance of the journalist as a figure in politics. Both, I will argue, are cause for alarm.

Meanwhile, disgust with the news media's performance has reemerged, with prominent journalists often leading the way. Here is a sample of some of the more provocative comments during the 1992 campaign: Max Frankel, executive editor of the *New York Times*, remarking on the Gennifer Flowers episode: "I'm quite ashamed for my profession."[7] Ward Just, a former correspondent for the *Washington Post* and now a novelist, denouncing "the worst political coverage in my adult memory" on the *Post*'s op-ed page: "The fourth branch of government, powerful, numerous, smug, prurient, protected by its own constitutional amendment, is behaving like a gang of arrogant rich kids at an out-of-town saloon, where anything goes and no one prosecutes."[8] Anthony Lewis of the *New York Times* during the New York primary campaign in April: "The American press prides itself on its courage, its selflessness, its influence. But in the current campaign those claims sound like a bad joke. The press is distinguished by its cynicism and its self-regard. Yes, it does have influence—for the worse."[9] Peter Jennings of ABC during the Democratic convention in July: "It hit me in New Hampshire when I realized that the press only cared about Gennifer Flowers and the voters only cared about the economy."[10] Sander Vanocur, veteran correspondent for NBC and ABC, at another roundtable during the same convention: "I think we're destroying the political structure of this country. We really should step back and think about what we're doing."[11] Finally, Thomas Oliphant of the *Boston Globe* offered this assessment in early June:

At halftime in the quadrennial national ordeal, it ought to be
clear that, along with the Republican and Democratic parties,
the other institution in deep doo-doo is journalism. To understand why, just think back over everything you have heard and
read about all the people who have run for president this
year, including the three sad souls who left the game. If you
think about this mass of material, one inescapable conclusion
emerges, based solely upon the press coverage—none of
these people deserves to be president because they are all fools,
liars, cheats, crooks, and failures. The truth, of course, is that
they are all human beings, with defects and strengths, good
ideas and bad ones, accomplishments and flops; but in the
distorting, supermagnification of modern media, the defects,
the bad ideas, and flops are news. Worse, the dominance of
"gotcha" stories, scandal and rumor-mongering is so great that
perspective (once the signal contribution of good journalism)
has been lost. . . .[12]

To be sure, many in the press feel that the coverage in 1992 has been
better than in 1988.[13] But the mix of shame, indignation, regret, self-reproach,
and alarm in the above comments deserves to be taken seriously.
Thoughtful journalists are increasingly aware that the tactic of aggressive confrontation with politicians has degenerated into something far
less useful—a "gotcha" routine that mostly serves the immediate interests of the press. At the same time, no responsible critic in or out of journalism wants the press to become uncritical and compliant, a mere delivery device for propaganda. How to acknowledge the truth in both of these
perceptions and move toward a new understanding of the journalist's task?

The essential problem is that the journalist's method of being critical is not disciplined by any political vision. It is not that the press is too
hard on politicians; rather, journalists have been too easy on themselves—
intellectually and politically. While they have a procedure for being critical—on display at any news conference—they have not found a project that would inform the use of that procedure. To proclaim a "project"
would, of course, be to advance a kind of agenda, and this is part of what
prevents the press from rethinking its approach. "All we own is our credibility," say many in the profession, and they interpret this to mean that
the press cannot afford to be caught with an agenda. At the same time,
however, they agree that it is the journalist's mission to be "tough" on
politicians and a persistent check on government power. The consequences of holding these two beliefs—no to an explicit agenda, yes to
a tough, critical stance—have been severe. The journalist's critical

method is degenerating into madness as "gotcha" becomes the battle cry of a hardened and increasingly purposeless press.

During the New York primary campaign in April, a media frenzy of uncommon intensity, Gail Collins of *Newsday* went well beyond "gotcha" when she announced her belief in "our God-given right to spend two weeks torturing the candidates to the best of our ability."[14] Absent the hyperbole, this describes well the prevailing attitude in the campaign press: politicians deserve whatever hell we put them through because they're politicians. To imagine a more useful routine than "torturing" political candidates will not be easy. Journalists will have to change more than their behavior—they will have to face the problem of belief. And they must learn to think of themselves, not only as a "factor" in politics, but as influential actors.

David Broder of the *Washington Post* is perhaps the nation's most respected political reporter. So it was of some interest when, in January 1990, he used his weekly column to address his colleagues in the national press. "We cannot allow the [November] elections to be another exercise in public disillusionment and political cynicism," Broder wrote. This was a startling sentence, for it saw journalists as answerable, not only for the reports they produce, but for the realities they report. "It is time for those of us in the world's freest press to become activists, not on behalf of a particular party or politician, but on behalf of the process of self-government," said Broder. He went on to add some specific advice: the campaign must be rescued from "the electronic demagoguery favored by too many hired-gun political consultants," who "collect their fees and go off to another campaign in another state." It is up to journalists "to step forward to police the campaign process, very much as we try to catch cheating and chicanery in government," Broder wrote:

> That means that we must be far more assertive than in the past on the public's right to hear its concerns discussed by the candidates—in ads, debates and speeches—and far more conscientious in reporting those discussions when they take place. We have to help reconnect politics and government—what happens in the campaign and what happens afterward in public policy—if we are to have accountability by our elected officials and genuine democracy in this country.[15]

Broder starts from the assumption that the press is a political instrument, a truism in politics since the eighteenth century. But he goes on to say that the instrument of the press should be employed by *journalists themselves* to alter and improve political debate. Here he crosses into uncharted territory. Broder wants his colleagues to become "activists ... on behalf of the process of self-government," to agree that they "cannot allow" the next election to repeat the destructive patterns of the past, to assume a professional duty to "reconnect politics and government." He asks them to acknowledge that they are not mere chroniclers of the political scene, but players in the game who can (and should) try to shape the outcome.

If journalists are seen as actors, it is reasonable to expect them to have an agenda—a desired outcome of their actions. Not only must they acknowledge an agenda; they must be able to persuade others—media owners, politicians, critics, the public—that their agenda is a proper one. They must find a language that justifies their project in terms the political community will accept. Another name for such a language is "rhetoric"—but rhetoric is a term of abuse among journalists who equate it with the phony claptrap that flows from politicians and their spokespeople.

What should the political agenda of the press be? How can journalists "sell" this agenda to wider audiences? What sort of rhetoric should they employ to describe their aims within politics? These questions confound the journalism profession's view of itself.

Journalists like to see themselves as observers; the pose they prefer is one of principled detachment. Their job is tell the truth, not to bring new truths into being. The press reports on what is happening in politics, questions officials and candidates, sounds the alarm about dangerous or controversial deeds, exposes corruption, and editorializes about current topics of concern. Almost all the key notions in the journalist's ethical code reflect an emphasis on detachment: the maligned but still influential doctrine of "objectivity," the related emphasis on "fairness" and "balance," the separation between the news columns and the editorial page, the "watchdog" role, the "adversarial" stance, the principle of ignoring consequences in deciding what's newsworthy. None of these ideas provides much guidance to the people Broder tried to address: professionals willing to acknowledge their influence in politics and to use it on behalf of "genuine democracy in this country."

In short, there is little in the outlook of the American journalist that even approaches a philosophy of action. But it is not only journalists who decline this challenge. It is the entire political culture and its preoccupation with media "bias." On the Left, the discourse on bias begins with the conviction that the "corporate media" is in league with the status quo—that it emphasizes official reality and marginalizes the Left and its critique of American society. On the Right, the charge is that the "liberal media" push an ideological agenda that is out of touch with mainstream America and plainly hostile to conservative views.[16] Scattered across the political spectrum are various interest groups that complain about their "image" in the media. African-Americans, for example, are angered at the frequency with which young blacks are shown on the news as criminals, hands cuffed and heads bowed. Anti-Asian bias, anti-Arab bias, bias against gays—all have their watchdog groups.

What these groups typically demand is "objectivity," "fairness," "balance," and "accuracy"—the very terms that leave journalists bereft of any philosophy of action.[17] The leading left-wing watchdog group calls itself Fairness and Accuracy in Reporting (FAIR). Among its declared aims is to "correct bias and imbalance" in the news. Accuracy in Media (AIM), a right-wing group, employs almost identical language. Its literature advocates "fairness, balance and accuracy in news reporting." The organizers of the Committee on Media Integrity (Comint), another right-wing group focusing on public television, say they are for "objectivity, fairness and balance in current affairs programming."[18]

It is significant that the rhetoric of "accuracy," "fairness," "balance," and "objectivity" is mandatory for what are clearly political pressure groups. For it indicates our general reluctance to take a political view of the journalist's task. There is reason for this reluctance. It's our way of saying that journalists should commit themselves to the truth, not to some preconceived notion of things or to some powerful interest's view of the world. But the duty to see things as they are belongs to everyone in a democracy. Vaclav Havel calls it "living in truth," one of the joys and prerequisites of a free society.[19] To live within the truth is not easy, of course, for we disagree about where the truth lies. But the truth is neither a particular responsibility nor an exclusive possession of the journalist—although some in the press forget this from time to time.

If a commitment to truth isn't particular to journalism, what kind of commitment is? This is the question objectivity and its various code words help everyone to avoid. It is the same question begged by critiques of media bias—namely, what sort of "bias" should we *ask* the press to display? Until we are ready to face this question, there will be no fundamental improvement in the journalist's treatment of politics, and each election year will bring another round of conferences that confirm the problems but lead to no lasting solutions.

To improve their coverage of politics, journalists must do more than tinker with their existing approach. They need to arrive at a vision of politics for which the practice of journalism clearly stands. They must try to imagine how politics would work when, according to their philosophy, it is working well. Broder began to suggest such a vision when he wrote of an "activist" press that would support, not a particular political result, but a particular kind of politics, which he calls the "process of self-government." But what does such a phrase mean beyond a vague commitment to democratic values?

Political philosopher Michael Sandel has written that "when politics goes well, we can know a good in common that we cannot know alone."[20] In my own thinking about the press and politics I have returned to Sandel's notion again and again, for it seems to me an ideal description of what journalists should commit themselves to—not this proposal or that plan, not the liberal agenda or the conservative cause, but a certain kind of discourse that permits the political community to understand itself in a better, fuller way. Journalists should try to make politics "go well," so that it produces a discussion in which the polity learns more about itself, its current problems, its real divisions, its place in time, its prospects for the future. By their commitment to such a discussion—and the sort of politics that would produce it—journalists might distinguish themselves from other actors and reclaim some of their lost authority in the American public sphere.

Let us give a name to the kind of politics I am describing. We can call it "public politics," a particular way of viewing the political scene. In public politics, the activity that is most visible is discussion and debate. Politics is seen as a continuing conversation, in which different rhetorics compete for influence, new debates arise and progress, emergent facts are given various interpretations, and arguments interact with events. This, I contend, is how journalists should view the political scene: they should grant privileged status to the metaphor of conversation. Politics as conversation is not the only possible lens on the political world, but it offers journalists the best way of understanding their task. Their job—an important one—is to improve the manner in which the political community converses with itself, so that the contest of politics brings a competition of ideas, and not only a clash of organized interests, clever tactics, or calculated images. Public politics, then, is a way that journalists can view the political scene so as to size up their opportunities for improving it.

In *electoral politics*, a different view of the same scene, the emphasis is on the struggle for votes and the piecing together of a winning majority. This is the way pollsters and campaign strategists define political reality. (And it is the perspective reporters adopt when they focus on the so-called horse race.) In *interest group politics*, another way of viewing the scene, the focus is on the zero-sum game of exerting pressure and influencing decisions. This is how lobbyists and their clients see things. In *image politics*, the point is to control the flow of media messages, to maintain a favorable impression in the public mind. This is the typical perspective of image advisers and "spin doctors." None of these perspectives is appropriate for the press because none offers the journalist a positive mission. Public politics does. It permits the press to try to advance the discussion the political community is having with itself.

Supposing they adopt this agenda, what sort of actions can journalists take to support political debate and to involve the public in the conversation? I discuss below an example of a local newspaper that took on these tasks. The newspaper's aim was not to bring about any particular policy result, but to revive public politics, to create new opportunities for political discussion and civic participation. The example also shows how journalists might go beyond a purely adversarial relationship to politicians and public life, without at the same time becoming mindless boosters of the status quo. The case of the Columbus, Georgia, *Ledger-Enquirer*, one I have discussed elsewhere,[21] bears on many of these themes: the journalist as political actor, Broder's notion of a political but not partisan "agenda," and the responsibility of the press to improve political discourse.

Columbus, a small city about one hundred miles southwest of Atlanta, did not share in the economic boom that came to much of the South in the 1970s and 1980s. Its economy, long dominated by the textile industry and nearby Fort Benning, had begun slowly to shift. More service industries were moving in, but it was unclear whether the schools could provide the sort of educated work force necessary for a high-wage economy. More middle-class people were arriving in Columbus, but the city lacked the amenities and civic improvements needed to hold these newcomers. The racial makeup of the community was also changing. Blacks had become a majority in the schools, and they were a third of all registered voters, but the political system had been slow in adjusting to these facts. There was still time to preserve an integrated school system, but the community was missing the leadership that might gradually shift power to the black majority while also preventing white flight.

There were other problems. New highway links were on the horizon, but the local roads that fed into these highways would have to be improved, and the tax money was unavailable. In 1982, the voters had sent a hostile message to local government, passing a referendum that placed a ceiling on the dollar amount of the municipal budget. It was later thrown out by the courts, but the hostility endured. In short, a familiar picture could be seen in Columbus: unmet needs, long-term problems, lack of vigorous leadership, no political will, and a general mistrust of government expressed through the tax code (conditions that resemble the state of national politics in 1992).

In 1987, the Columbus newspaper, the *Ledger-Enquirer*, owned by the Knight-Ridder chain, decided to do something about the problem. The editors planned a series of articles that would examine the future of the city and the issues the citizenry needed to confront. The paper surveyed the views of local residents about their community and what they wanted it to become. A team of reporters conducted in-depth interviews with residents in their homes, while other correspondents spoke to experts in a variety of fields. The research was put together in a package, called "Columbus: Beyond 2000," which appeared in eight parts in the spring of 1988.

The report showed that most residents of Columbus liked their city and wanted to remain there. But it warned of a host of persistent difficulties. These included transportation bottlenecks, a history of low wages in the local economy, lack of nightlife in the city, a faltering school system, and the perception that a local elite had dominated city politics to the exclusion of all others. If the journalists at the *Ledger-Enquirer* had stopped there, they could have congratulated themselves on their efforts. They had offered the community a thorough and reasonably sophisticated portrait of itself and its problems. But they did not stop there.

After the series was published, the editors waited for the reactions to come in. But after a period of brief chatter, the series was met with silence and inaction. It is not hard to see why. The problems the newspaper had identified were serious, but they had the defect of being gradual. They could easily be ignored for another day, month, or year. They were problems that might involve difficult choices and require some vision to address—in short, the sorts of issues governments avoid unless pressured. The *Ledger-Enquirer* had tried to exert pressure through its report and some strongly worded editorials. But these measures emerged into a kind of political vacuum. The community lacked organization, leadership, debate. It had a government, but it lacked politics—"public politics."

This was the first challenge Columbus had to address. Before it could meet the challenge of preparing for its future, it had to face the immediate problem of a missing public debate. The *Ledger-Enquirer* had sought to contribute to such a debate with its eight-part series. But it discovered that the debate did not exist, so it took a further step: it organized a town meeting where residents could discuss the future of their city. The meeting created a public space for the emergence of a widespread sentiment: that there was plenty to do in Columbus and plenty of people who wanted to see something done. Three hundred citizens showed up for six hours of talk. They came from diverse backgrounds, and many had never participated in public life before. Journalists helped to run the meeting, but they rarely spoke. Their purpose was to provide a forum for citizens to speak. And what the citizens spoke about was not the incinerator proposed for their backyard but their concerns about the future of their city and the way it was run.

Shortly after the town meeting, the editor of the newspaper, the late Jack Swift, organized a barbeque at his home for seventy-five interested citizens. Out of that gathering came a new civic organization, called United Beyond 2000. The group was headed by a thirteen-member steering committee, of which Swift was the leading member. Thus, in the person of the editor there was a direct and visible tie between the newspaper and this new community group. A number of task forces sprang up to address specific issues. These included recreation needs, child-care issues, race relations, and the special problems of teenagers. All were staffed by citizen volunteers. Their goal was not to lobby for specific policies, but to encourage average citizens as well as influential people to talk to each other, in the hope that they would choose to work together for change.

Among the changes Columbus needed was a new climate for race relations, which were still affected by a history of segregation and the memory of brutal violence. Swift, the white newspaper editor, had made friends with John Allen, a black state court judge. The two friends decided that, as citizens, they could do something about the race problem in Columbus. They began to hold backyard barbeques at their own homes, to which each man would invite a dozen or so friends. There was no agenda at these meetings, but there was an idea behind them: to bring together people of different races who ordinarily would not meet, in hopes that they would discover common interests or at least develop a mutual respect. At each barbeque, a small number of newcomers were invited so that the group would continue to expand. This "friendship network," as the project was called, grew to include some 250 members, from white bank executives to black barbershop owners.

The United Beyond 2000 group went on to sponsor other public events, including a town meeting that drew 400 young people to a local mall for a discussion of their common concerns. The teenagers later organized their own mayoral forum, the first debate ever held between candidates for mayor in Columbus. The success of the movement in Columbus began to impress citizens in other cities around the region, who then sought to organize themselves in a similar fashion. Meanwhile, the newspaper continued to hammer away at the city's failure to come up with a clear agenda for the future. It reported at length on the lack of strategic planning in local government. It explained how other cities of a similar size were trying to think about the long term. It continued to do "tough" reporting, but it attempted to be constructively tough.

About a year after the publication of the original eight-part series, the Columbus city manager dragged himself and a few aides into Jack Swift's office. He acknowledged that the newspaper was right: the city had failed to develop a forward-looking agenda. But this would soon be remedied, he told Swift. The city manager then planned a series of retreats where city council members and other officials could come to grips with the problems Columbus would face in the years ahead. Out of these retreats came a new strategic plan for the city. At the same time, the community group continued to push the message of inclusiveness. It reminded the city fathers that those who had always been excluded in the past would have to have some say when decisions were made about the future.

So the newspaper and the civic movement worked in tandem, and they accomplished at least three things: First, they opened up the political process to more people and got public discussion going again. Second, they created an informal network of social contacts that broke down race and class barriers and prepared the way for a larger coalition. Third, and most relevant to the present discussion, they managed to alter the location of politics, shifting it toward the public sphere to involve more citizens. A related goal was to alter the time frame of politics, moving it forward so that Columbus could grapple now with what it desired to become in the future.

What Jack Swift and his colleagues also did was reimagine the position of the journalist in politics. Instead of standing outside the political community and reporting on its pathologies, they took up residence within its borders. This was a courageous move that made a difference to the citizens of Columbus. And it aided the newspaper in its relationship to the city. As noted earlier, journalists often fear that abandoning their detached position will cost them their credibility. But as the *Ledger-Enquirer*'s publisher, Billy Watson, observed, "The biggest credibility problem we have is that we're viewed as arrogant, negative and detached from the community, as tearing the community down." The United Beyond 2000 project "did more to enhance the credibility and reputation of the newspaper than anything we've done," Watson said.[22]

What is significant about the *Ledger-Enquirer*'s experiment is not the organization of a few town meetings. They were merely a means to an end. The end was a different kind of politics, in which public discussion and civic involvement could play a larger part. This became the newspaper's project—political but not partisan. Not only did Knight-Ridder not veto the experiment; it promoted the Columbus initiative as an exemplary case of community involvement.[23]

In retrospect, the turning point in the *Ledger-Enquirer*'s experiment was when its enterprising series on the future of the city drew no visible response. The editors then had to interpret this reaction. They could have felt perversely vindicated, confirmed in the cynical view that those in power care nothing for the city's future and want only to preserve the status quo or to win the next election. Another possibility was to doubt the influence and prestige of the newspaper, and thus by implication their own authority—that is, the editors might have said to themselves, "Why should Columbus jump when we say jump?" A third possibility was to see the lack of response as a legitimate expression of public opinion: "Look, we tried, but our readers just aren't interested."

A fourth interpretation is the one Swift and others at the newspaper actually chose: to be disturbed when a call for action produces nothing but silence. By their willingness to be disturbed in this way they showed a certain confidence in their own authority, in the quality of their work, and in the rightness of their concern for a community that, in their view, could not afford to remain complacent and inert. Behind the *Ledger-Enquirer*'s initiative, then, was an important moral proposition: that it is wrong for communities to drift without direction when the future is closing in on them. In a democracy, the remedy for this condition is politics. To insist that politics assume its proper functions was the "cause" the newspaper adopted.[24]

The arena in which the *Ledger-Enquirer* took action was a limited one—a city small enough where face-to-face dialogue could still make a difference. In national politics the challenge is obviously different. Here the press cannot be expected to assemble a public of 250 million. But what it can do is take on the task of improving political discourse and the climate of public debate. This is what Broder had in mind in an article he wrote around the same time as his 1990 column. He presented his colleagues with a "five-point agenda" for the next election:

▲   Take the campaign agenda away from the consultants and handlers who are interested only in the hot-button themes that might win the election. Replace it with a "voters' agenda" to be determined through reporters' interviews with average citizens about what really concerns them. Push this agenda in press conferences, campaign stops, and election-year coverage.

▲ Remind people of vicious and distorting ads they saw in previous campaigns as a way of suggesting to consultants that any decision to "go negative" would bring a public backlash.

▲ Treat ads and direct mailings like campaign speeches or policy statements; interrogate candidates about them.

▲ Investigate ads, demand evidence for claims made in them, report lies and evasions "in plain language."

▲ In editorials and columns, regularly denounce "those who sabotage the election process by their paid-media demagoguery."

Broder's wish list is plainly a political agenda—but not only because it deals with election-year politics. It is "political" in a far deeper sense of the word. Politics is an arena of contest and conflict, where competing visions of the good do battle with one another. Broder not only offers his colleagues such a vision; he is blunt about the opponents who will have to be defeated for this vision to triumph. The opponents, in his view, are the campaign consultants and handlers (and the candidates under their influence) who define "politics" in an unacceptably narrow way—as the process of winning elections.[25]

To Broder this is a false vision. He offers his own: politics as the process by which the ideal of "self-government" becomes a living reality, the means by which a free people decide on their concerns, communicate them to government, and pressure government to respond. Journalists, he says, should fight to see that this vision of politics triumphs in the next election. They should become "activists . . . on behalf of the process of self-government." They will undoubtedly be opposed. But this should not deter them. Broder writes: "We [in the press] have been inhibited by thinking that if we did any more, we would be thought partisan. But we need to become partisan—not on behalf of a candidate or a party—but on behalf of the process."[26]

These urgings go against the natural temperament of most journalists, which is to be "against" rather than "for." Journalists are proud of their oppositional stance, especially in relation to office-seekers and office-holders. It is their willingness to be tough (on everyone, they say) that makes them valuable to the political community—or so they think. "Toughness" might even be considered the default agenda of the press, an end in itself to be pursued regardless of consequences. This would help to explain the feeding frenzy, which is usually seen as a regrettable by-product of a competitive spirit. An alternative explanation would focus on journalists' inflated need to be "against" in the absence of something to be "for." Lacking any positive mission or approved agenda, journalists seek an agreed-upon target for the mutual exhibition of their toughness. The feeding frenzy is like a hazing ritual that helps those doing the hazing know who they are. They're the press because they demand honest answers to difficult questions, defined as those that threaten the candidate with the most damage. Roger Ailes, media adviser to Presidents Reagan and Bush, caught the essence of this pattern when he said to a reporter, "You get up every morning and try to humiliate my client. I get up every morning and try to make him look good. I sleep better."[27]

The journalist's urge—or is it a need?—to wound and humiliate may also be a reaction to the routines of daily newswork, which cause reporters to become neurotically dependent on the very same officials they try to dismember when a gaffe occurs or scandal strikes. Resenting their regular manipulation by politicians and handlers, journalists strike back where they can, trying to humble the people they must otherwise beg for news. The dangers of this pattern have not been fully appreciated. Over time, the feeding frenzy and the cult of toughness may actually wear away at the spot that attaches the First Amendment to the profession of journalism. This is illustrated by one of the most interesting moments of the campaign season, which occurred during Bill Clinton's April 1 appearance on Phil Donahue's show.

Clinton agreed to appear on "Donahue" during the height of the hazing the Democratic candidates endured in New York. His host decided to greet him with thirty minutes of questions about an alleged affair with Gennifer Flowers and other assorted inquiries into his "character." Clinton tried to resist. He told Donahue that such tactics were "debasing our politics." He said, "You are responsible for the cynicism in this country. You don't want to talk about the real issues." But Donahue persisted, demanding to know if Clinton was denying the allegations or merely contesting Donahue's right to ask about them. This brought groans from the audience and cries of "Oh come on! Get off it! Enough!" Donahue did move on—to Clinton's marijuana use and his marital difficulties. When the show returned from a commercial break, Donahue ventured into the studio audience for questions. The first questioner was twenty-five-year-old Melissa Roth, who later said she was a Republican. Her remarks were delivered with intensity and aimed at Donahue:

> I think really given the pathetic state of most of the United States at this point—Medicare, education, everything else—I can't believe you spent half an hour of air time attacking this man's character. I'm not even a Bill Clinton supporter, but I think this is ridiculous.[28]

This brought a loud ovation from the audience, most of whom appeared to share her frustration.

There are several things worth noting about this episode. First, while Donahue is generally considered a television personality rather than a journalist, and while he often must cope with condescending criticism from the "serious" press, in this case he was doing exactly what many journalists would do. He was pressing Clinton for answers about the "character" issues that were then dominating press coverage of the campaign. He was refusing to allow the candidate's denials to pass without aggressive follow-ups. He was exhibiting his toughness by probing the areas he knew that Clinton wanted to avoid. In short, he was behaving exactly as Lesley Stahl or Sam Donaldson might behave, to name two television journalists noted for their aggressive style. This is important because the audience's reaction to Donahue can be interpreted as a reaction against the journalist's mindset in these situations, even though the situation lacked a "real" journalist.

Second, critics and journalists have grown accustomed to "explaining" the excesses of the media by reference to the audience's alleged appetite for gossip and entertainment. The encounter on the "Donahue" show confounded this explanation, for it was Donahue alone who appeared to display the appetite for further inquiry into the candidate's private life. In pressuring Clinton to come clean about his alleged infidelity, Donahue was not, in fact, representing the interests of his audience, which lay elsewhere. But what he did represent—and represent well—was the cult of toughness in professional journalism, the journalist's belief in a "God-given right to spend two weeks torturing the candidates," as Gail Collins put it.

Whatever one may think of this "right," it does have some basis in law. After the landmark case of *New York Times v. Sullivan* (1964)— which made it extremely difficult for public figures to prevail in libel suits—journalists can plausibly claim a kind of "right to torture" any public official or candidate. But not even the Constitution can protect the press against the public fallout from the repeated exercise of this right. The fallout hit when Melissa Roth started scolding Donahue. As the audience applauded her outburst, Clinton broke into a confident smile, while Donahue, somewhat taken back, stood alone, isolated within a studio normally under his firm control. We might also say that journalism stood alone, bereft of public support or cultural authority. Here was an instance when the journalist's sacred battle cry, the "public's right to know," became the public's battle cry *against* the journalist. By refusing to question Clinton about the public's true business—"Medicare, education, everything else"—Donahue had unwittingly forfeited the First Amendment authority journalists believe is theirs for life.

In discussions of the First Amendment, members of the press often betray a belief that freedom of the press somehow belongs to them, as if the Founding Fathers had meant to single out an occupational group for special status in the republic. Many journalists seem unaware that there is an entire tradition of thinking about the free press clause that puts primary emphasis, not on the rights of the press, but on the citizen's right to adequate information and vigorous public debate.[29] In certain contexts this right may be upheld against the managers of the media and their desire to do as they please. The primary text for this interpretation is the Supreme Court's decision in *Red Lion Broadcasting Co. v. FCC* (1969), a case that upheld the government's right to regulate broadcasters.

As First Amendment scholar Lee C. Bollinger observes in his recent work, *Images of a Free Press*, "To read the Court's unanimous opinion in *Red Lion* is to step into another world, one that encompasses a dramatically different way of thinking about the press and the role of public regulation. . . ." In this other world, it is the media that is seen as "the most serious threat to the ultimate First Amendment goal, the creation of an intelligent and informed democratic electorate." Government regulation ensures that the media will meet its responsibilities to the citizenry. Bollinger quotes the relevant passages in the Court's opinion, in which the justices noted:

> It is the right of the public to receive suitable access to social, political, esthetic, moral and other ideas and experiences which is crucial here. That right may not be abridged either by Congress or by the FCC.[30]

As the argument in *Red Lion* suggests, there is nothing "God-given," or constitutionally ordained, about an arrangement in which the journalist represents the public by asking tough questions of those in power. Another alliance could easily arise, in which the state represents the public's interest in having "suitable access to social, political, esthetic, moral and other ideas and experiences," as the Supreme Court put it. What transpired in Donahue's studio was a sudden shift in this direction: rather than Donahue representing the audience's interests to Clinton, it became the audience representing their own interest to Donahue, with Clinton, a potential chief executive of the state, as the beneficiary. Behind his wan smile Clinton may have sensed the power of this moment, when the moral and political authority in "the public's right to know" slid over to him as a candidate for public office.

This is not to suggest that the journalist's constitutional protections are about to crumble because of one incident on the "Donahue" show. But I am arguing that those protections alone are not enough to guarantee the cultural authority and privileged position of the journalist in the political sphere. If the rise of the call-in show format means anything, it means that many viewers see no purpose in having the journalist intervene in politics. Max in Seattle feels as well represented by Julie's question from Houston as he would be by Sam Donaldson's inquiry from New York. While this has been interpreted (by Broder, among others) as healthy competition for a complacent press, there is another way of looking at it.[31]

Despite their presence on-screen for some thirty years of the television age, journalists have somehow been unable to convince a large portion of the audience that they are necessary to politics. Why is this? The reason, I think, is that they advance a weak and unconvincing argument to explain why they're necessary. It amounts, again, to a celebration of the cult of toughness: ordinary people are too polite to ask rude questions about sensitive subjects, or to follow up when politicians fail to answer. If this is all journalists can offer the political community—a level of shamelessness and aggression that ordinary people cannot manage—then it is easy to see why the offer is refused. One can predict that more and more Americans will refuse it as other avenues for political discourse emerge. Call-in shows, talk radio, C-Span, 800 numbers, videos and pamphlets produced by candidates for voters—all promise information and political dialogue without intervention by journalists.

As Paul Taylor argues in this volume, there is much that is healthy and democratic about an increasing array of direct links between voters and politicians. But the press ought to see in the current campaign, and especially in the Donahue incident, a warning: politics without journalists is a prospect we have glimpsed this year, and for the moment it looks rather good.[32] Those in the press who applaud the call-in phenomenon exhibit a democratic impulse, a trust in the good sense of the citizenry, that should itself be applauded.[33] But there is another issue here, and it has to do with the authority of the journalist as a figure in politics. If journalists cannot convince the rest of us that they belong on-screen, that they are worth listening to, that they add something to public discourse that would be missing if they were not there, then the press will lose an asset of inestimable value: not only the attention of television viewers but the public support it needs to remain free and independent.

Journalists are fond of quoting the Founding Fathers on the importance of a free press. One father they rarely get around to quoting is Alexander Hamilton, who actually said the most on the subject in the Federalist essays. In the Federalist No. 84 Hamilton wrote:

> What is the liberty of the press? Who can give it any definition which would not leave the utmost latitude for evasion? I hold it to be impracticable; and from this I infer, that its security, whatever fine declarations may be inserted in any constitution respecting it, must altogether depend on public opinion, and on the general spirit of the people and of the government.

Nowadays we think we know better than Hamilton. We believe that liberty of the press has been well protected by the Constitution, and we celebrate the Bill of Rights as one of the great political achievements of humankind. We are right to celebrate, but we are wrong to overlook the wisdom in what Hamilton was saying.

The American press is generally regarded as the freest in the world. But often it is not the Constitution that grants this freedom. It is "the general spirit of the people and of the government," as Hamilton wrote. We saw a clear demonstration of this during the Persian Gulf War. Journalists were unanimous in denouncing the restrictions the Pentagon placed on them during the fighting. They complained bitterly about the military's tight control over access and information, as they did following the invasions of Grenada in 1983 and Panama in 1989.[34] But in all these cases there was almost no outcry from the American public about the restrictions; nor did officials in government, moved by their conscience, lobby for a change in the Pentagon's policy, or resign in protest when the controls continued.[35]

In their struggle to free themselves from state interference, journalists could not count on the support of public opinion, which appeared to be against them. During the Gulf War the NBC comedy program "Saturday Night Live" began with a short sketch lampooning the questions reporters had been asking at daily briefings. The journalists were portrayed as ignorant, arrogant, and pointlessly adversarial. They said things like, "Are we planning an amphibious invasion of Kuwait, and if so, where exactly would that be?" By gently rebuffing their ludicrous questions, the Pentagon briefer came off as a model of sanity (this on a show not known for its kind treatment of government officials). The next Monday, White House Chief of Staff John Sununu overheard staffers chatting about the skit. He quickly ordered a tape of the program, and showed it to President Bush. According to an account by Jason

DeParle in the *New York Times*, the White House saw the "Saturday Night Live" skit as evidence that the government was outmaneuvering the press in the battle for public support. Freed from doubts about a possible backlash, the White House and the Pentagon decided to keep the press on a tight leash during the war. Now that "Saturday Night Live" was on their side, they could be confident that the television audience was, as well.[36]

The Pentagon had succeeded in getting the audience to identify with its representatives, while the press had not. Sensing this, the producers of "Saturday Night Live" decided that the journalists should be shown as the jerks, that it was their questions, and not the Pentagon's answers, that deserved ridicule. The comedy sketch not only picked up on this widespread feeling, but returned it to the audience with a stamp of approval: the performance of the press was now officially laughable. In essence, then, the press suffered a political defeat during the war. In a contest for public support, it lost, and the loss had a direct effect on journalists' freedom to report what was happening. This is one of the many reasons journalists should learn to think of themselves as political actors; others, including the occupants of the Pentagon and the White House, already think this way, and they act upon the press for what are clearly political reasons.

In 1991 I participated in three conferences on the press and the Gulf War. At all these meetings, correspondents and editors were virtually unanimous in agreeing that they "lost" the war. But the battle they believed they lost involved their struggle with the Pentagon over the rules for reporting the conflict. Their focus was almost exclusively on the details of pool arrangements and other restraints on reporters. The journalists believe, in other words, that the important relationship they have is with the Pentagon, rather than with the audience. The problem they want to solve involves the terms on which they will be allowed to report the next war.[37] But the real problem, I would suggest, is the terms on which they presented themselves to viewers at home.

Let us take the spectacle of the press briefings from Saudi Arabia. Frustrated by their inability to get into the field, inexperienced, in many cases, in military matters, and overly impressed with the value of the "tough" question, journalists were unable to communicate to the audience any sense that it was being served by reporters' inquiries. As Henry Allen of the *Washington Post* observed:

> The Persian Gulf press briefings are making reporters look like fools, nit-pickers and egomaniacs; like dilettantes who have spent exactly none of their lives on the end of a gun or even a shovel; dinner party commandos, slouching inquisitors,

collegiate spitball artists; people who have never been in a fist-
fight, much less combat; a whining, self-righteous, upper-mid-
dle class mob jostling for whatever tiny flakes of fame may set-
tle on their shoulders. . . .[38]

This unfortunate scene made it impossible for journalists to gener-
ate any image of authority. Ordinarily, the authority of the reporter resides
in a claim to have seen the events the rest of us can't witness. The
reporter says to us, "I was there, you weren't, let me tell you about it."
But in the briefings during the Gulf War, it was the military that was able
to say, "We're there, you're not, so let us tell you about it." In a sense,
then, the reporter's function shifted to the Pentagon briefers. The people who stood before us and told us about the war were people wear-
ing uniforms. The journalists were reduced to asking useless or unin-
formed questions.

Here is one of the lessons of the Gulf War for the press: in the video
age, the figure of the reporter is up for grabs. It can easily be grabbed
by government, as it was during the briefings from the Gulf. Is there
anything wrong with an arrangement in which the government serves
as both the conductor and reporter of the war? Journalists think so, and
they're right. But it's the public, not the Pentagon, that they need to persuade. From a television viewer's perspective, the Pentagon was more
convincing as a reporter of the war—and not only because it had more
information. It also had conviction: it wanted to win. What did journalists want? "To know" is perhaps the best answer they can give. It
is a decent, even noble answer, but it may be time to realize that it is
also incomplete.

On television, the demand to know is experienced in dramatic terms,
which means that those issuing the demand must convince us of their
sincerity and dedication. In posing aggressive questions to reluctant officials, the journalist is placed in the subliminal company of the court-
room attorney or the private detective—two figures in the popular
imagination who, like the press, must interrogate others to get at the
truth. But note the differences between these types. The attorneys on,
say, "L.A. Law" can be merciless in grilling a hostile witness. But later
in the show we see them mount an eloquent plea on their client's
behalf. They get to display their passions (and their considerable
rhetorical skills) in the closing arguments that are such a prominent feature of "L.A. Law." These scenes help to redeem the earlier interrogations, for we can see that all that aggressiveness had a point—summarized
in the attorney's thesis about what actually happened, and in the final
plea for an innocent (or guilty) verdict. In televised journalism, we

rarely see the ritual of the interrogation redeemed in this way: the thesis never comes, the plea is not permitted. The aggressiveness of the press can thus seem pointless—a theatrical display of animus and suspicion.[39]

In the figure of the detective we find any number of dramatic parallels to the journalist—the hard-boiled exterior, the overfamiliarity with lies and deceit, the mistrust of others' motives, the lack of any personal or political commitment, the dogged pursuit of a hidden truth. These traits were captured for all time in the screen persona of Humphrey Bogart. Bogart, of course, was a great actor, which meant that he could project through his evident bitterness a powerful sense of pain and loss. Watching him, we always have the sense that he suffered a tragic disappointment somewhere in the mists of the past. Eric Sevareid and Edward R. Murrow of CBS had a touch of this heroic sadness in their television personas, but in someone like Chris Wallace of ABC, one exemplar of today's adversarial style, there is no trace of suffering, no hint of a man forcibly stripped of his illusions. It is impossible to experience Chris Wallace as world-weary. Like his colleagues, he is weary of the claptrap he expects to hear from the politicians he interviews. So are many of his viewers, but by anticipating and confirming our own impatience with empty rhetoric Wallace fails to convince us that his interrogations have any point. He seems not to expect—to have ever expected—that things could be any different. Why should we respect him any more than the people who evade his questions?

It is all too easy (though often necessary) to condemn excessive cynicism in the press. My point is somewhat different: journalists on television tend to display a cynicism that feels false, superficial, unearned. They do not come off as disappointed believers. Nor do they seem like aggressive advocates of a just cause. They appear instead as a chorus of doubters, professional cynics who, despite their clever questions, know even less than we do about the real world and its disappointments—as Henry Allen put it, "collegiate spitball artists."

My argument is not that journalists must find a persona to match Bogart's. It is that "toughness" and the adversarial stance are simply not enough; nor is the pledge to deliver fair and accurate information. Journalists need a more compelling public function. But first they will have to decide, not only who they are "against," but what they are "for." They need a vision of the way they want politics and public discussion to go, and a commitment to make this vision a reality. My suggestion has been that journalists present themselves as advocates for the kind of serious talk a mature polity requires. They should practice this talk themselves, and not just condemn others for failing to engage in it. They should make active use of their power to publicize and promote some kinds of talk, while downgrading and ignoring others. They should announce and publicly defend their legitimate agenda: to make politics "go well," in the sense of producing a useful dialogue, where we can know in common what we cannot know alone, and where the true problems of the political community come under serious discussion.

Those in politics committed to such a discussion deserve the attention and respect of the press—imbalanced treatment, if you will. Those who undermine the conditions in which politics might "go well" deserve to be carefully criticized, or purposefully ignored. In their interrogations of public figures, journalists should be probing and critical, but they should also understand that their authority in these matters must be earned. It will be earned only if journalists can demonstrate a belief in—and a talent for—a better, richer political dialogue, one they are continually striving to imagine. To undertake this act of imagination they will have to change their lens on the political world and learn to see politics anew, as a discussion they have a duty to improve. But first, of course, the press must acknowledge the existence of an old lens, a manner of viewing politics that has gradually broken down, making it more and more difficult for journalists to see their way clear of some destructive patterns. The horse race, insider baseball, the gotcha question, the feeding frenzy, the cult of toughness—these ought to be seen as unsustainable practices (to employ an ecological metaphor).

In thinking about what keeps these practices in place, one cannot avoid the influence of opinion polling on the press. Journalists made a mistake years ago when they more or less accepted the results of polls as their working definition of public opinion. The mistake had little to do with the familiar problems involving volatility, reliability, and margin of error in polling. These are technical matters. By getting into the business of measuring public opinion, journalists abandoned their duty to improve it. This, I believe, was their mistake. One way to correct it is to take seriously an idea advanced by Daniel Yankelovich, a leading pollster and cofounder of the Public Agenda Foundation, a nonprofit group that studies public opinion and its potential improvement.

Yankelovich argues that public judgment should succeed public opinion in the journalist's prestige rankings (and in the political culture as a whole). By public judgment he means "the state of highly developed public opinion that exists once people have engaged an issue, considered it from all sides, understood the choices it leads to, and accepted the full consequences of the choices they make." In explaining the concept, he writes:

> Most expressions of public opinion, as measured in opinion polls, do not reflect public judgment. For example, opinion polls report that Americans believe the threat of global warming to be of the utmost gravity, so much so that people say the nation should not wait for scientific proof to take far-reaching remedial action. And yet, these same studies also show that Americans are unwilling to consider even modest sacrifices or changes in life-style. . . . This specimen of public opinion is not public judgment. Rather, it is merely a snapshot of public opinion at a moment in time caught in the turmoil of grappling with an abstract threat that is not yet real and that Americans have not genuinely engaged. Two years from now, or five, or twenty years from now, events may force the public to confront the issue more fully, struggle with the pain of hard choices, and make a fateful decision to accept the changes needed to counter the threat. Then we will have public judgment.[40]

The notion of public judgment gives the press something to be "for" in the realm of public opinion. At present, we speak of public opinion as a kind of verdict: yes or no, approve or disapprove, favorable or unfavorable. This is the concept of opinion the polls enforce. Understood as a verdict, public opinion provides nothing for the journalist to do except measure and interpret the results. We don't want the press to be "for" a particular verdict as against another—to be in favor of a lower (or higher) approval rating for the president, for example. Journalists know this, and it confirms their intention to take a neutral attitude toward public opinion. Polling is their instrument of neutrality, their declaration of independence from all campaigns to shape or influence the verdict of public opinion. That does not mean that the polls themselves are neutral, or have no political effects. Rather, journalists use polling to sever themselves from the political community, to stand outside its deliberations, to flatten it into something they can "survey."

Suppose, then, we understand public opinion not as a verdict, but as a process by which a political community comes to understand and debate its choices. Under this definition the press has an important task: to improve the chances that public opinion will evolve into public judgment. Yankelovich entitled his book *Coming to Public Judgment: Making Democracy Work in a Complex World* to emphasize the evolution of public opinion from one state to another. Thus, instead of telling us "what the public thinks," the press might focus more on how a public comes to "think"—that is, the process by which a political community forms public judgments out of a mass of opinions.

Yankelovich makes an essential contribution when he criticizes the common view that adding "information," especially the advice of experts, is the best way to improve public opinion. He argues instead that the "quality" of public opinion reflects the way people approach public issues—their ability to think clearly about values, priorities, and consequences—rather than the amount of information they have.[41] The real challenge in improving public opinion is not to add more information, or to grab public attention for a neglected issue. It is to encourage people to state their concerns, clarify their values, order their priorities, and appreciate the consequences of the views they hold. These improvements can come only through the process of deliberation and debate. By participating in this process—and by watching debate being conducted in an exemplary fashion—citizens stand a chance of improving their opinions, and learning the art of political judgment.

"What democracy requires is public debate, not information," wrote historian and social critic Christopher Lasch in 1990. Lasch continued:

> Of course, it needs information, too, but the kind of information it needs can be generated only by vigorous popular debate. We do not know what we need to know until we ask the right questions, and we can ask the right questions only by subjecting our own ideas about the world to the test of public controversy. Information, usually seen as the precondition of debate, is better-understood as its by-product. When we get into arguments that focus and fully engage our attention, we become avid seekers of relevant information. Otherwise we take in information passively—if we take it in at all.

Lasch concludes that "the job of the press is to encourage debate, not to supply the public with information."[42] He has it exactly right. Journalism is one of the arts of public life, but it is not the art of gathering news or torturing politicians. What skilled journalists must do is construct the political universe so that our discussion about it makes a difference. They must view politics as an arena for vigorous debate, and they should fight to uphold this vision against other competing (and hostile) views. Politics as a football game, politics as a struggle for votes, politics as a battle of interest groups, politics as a contest of personalities, politics as a scene of corruption and vice, politics as "another name for warfare" (as Lasch has written)—these are some of the visions that compete with the ideal of politics as public debate.[43] They all have their advocates and their temptations, and among those they tempt is the press.

But the press must remain virtuous. It can do so by holding to a vision of a political universe where conversation and dialogue have a central place—where what the polity needs to discuss does actually get discussed; where conflicting interests contend, not as hostile armies, but as compelling ideas; where personality, or "character," is disclosed through the ordeal of debate rather than the arrangement of imagery or the frenzy of a media-induced scandal; where to corrupt public discourse is an offense to the political community, while a genuinely useful contribution to debate is rewarded with the community's attention. Here is an "agenda" worth having, a politics worth dreaming of, and bringing about. It is the politics Broder advocated, the politics the Columbus *Ledger-Enquirer* tried to support, the politics Melissa Roth was missing on "Donahue," the politics we all missed in 1988 and are missing again in 1992.

I will close by repeating the questions I have tried to pose throughout. As actors within politics, what should journalists be trying to achieve? What ought to be on their agenda? What principles can guide the construction of that agenda? What sort of language might explain and justify those principles?

These questions have less to do with behavior than belief. Ultimately, journalists will have to decide what they believe in strongly enough to become "activists" on its behalf. Journalism is generally a doubting trade, not a believing one. The public warrant to doubt what others say and do may be part of what attracts people to the culture of the newsroom. Often, it seems, the journalist is the one who reveals the truth, and wrecks our hopes—including the hopes that collect around a candidate for public office.

In a February opinion column, Randolph Ryan of the *Boston Globe* took note of this attitude among his colleagues. "We truth-tellers at the ramparts should acknowledge a journalistic glee in helping front-runners stumble, making races more interesting. Some should also admit that they fear being seen as naive."[44] The fear Ryan cites is real, but he is one of the few in his profession with the courage to admit it. To be seen as naive is to be dismissed by most of those in the professional culture of journalism, where there is nothing more contemptible than a "true believer." With this attitude journalists cure themselves of any lingering faith that might discipline their fascination with politics. As a result their fascination turns negative, and truth-telling becomes an exercise in trashing facades.

The cure for this condition is what might be called a second naivete. It differs from the first, which is an unavoidable aspect of our youth. Our second naivete comes when we realize, as adults, that seeing through things doesn't always mean that we see them well. Without a vision, a positive glimpse of a possible world, our efforts to see clearly merely doom us to disenchantment. Journalists, being human, are not exempt from this truth, and I cannot imagine why they would want to be.

Notes

1. For observations by journalists on the decay of politics in the United States, see E.J. Dionne, Jr., *Why Americans Hate Politics* (New York: Simon & Schuster, 1991) and Michael Oreskes, "American Politics Loses Its Way As Its Vision Changes World," *New York Times*, March 18, 1990, p. A1. See also Robert Entman, *Democracy Without Citizens: Media and the Decline of American Politics* (New York: Oxford University Press, 1989).

2. Jon Katz, "Rock, Rap and Movies Bring You the News," *Rolling Stone*, March 5, 1992.

3. As one study puts it, "Traditionally, the press has asserted that it is the candidates who shape a campaign, that newspapers and television reflect a campaign's tone but do not set it. In the aftermath of 1988, however, journalists themselves have joined the ranks of those wondering about whether they are among those culpable for the decline of American political discourse." *Restoring the Bond: Connecting Campaign Coverage to Voters: A Report of the Campaign Lessons for '92 Project* (Cambridge, Mass.: Joan Shorenstein Barone Center on the Press, Politics and Public Policy, Harvard University, 1991), pp. 4, 5. On the 1988 campaign generally and the news media's role, see the report of the Markle Commission on the Media and the Electorate (New York: John & Mary R. Markle Foundation, 1990).

4. On news organizations' plans to change their coverage in 1992 given the experience of 1988, see Thomas B. Rosenstiel, "Coverage beyond the Sound Bite," *Los Angeles Times*, November 29, 1991; for a summary of the "lessons of 1988," see *Covering the Presidential Primaries* (New York: Freedom Forum Media Studies Center, Columbia University, 1992), p. 28.

5. Larry J. Sabato, *Feeding Frenzy: How Attack Journalism Has Transformed American Politics* (New York: Free Press, 1991). On Clinton and coverage of the character issues, see Thomas B. Rosenstiel, "Clinton Allegation Raises Questions on the Media's Role," *Los Angeles Times*, January 29, 1992, p. A1; Howard Kurtz, "Reports on Clinton Pose Quandary for Journalists," *Washington Post*, January 30, 1992, p. A14; John Tierney, "Now, Journalists Renege on Election Promises," *New York Times*, January 31, 1992, p. A1; Amy E. Schwartz, "Endless Questions," *Washington Post*, January 29, 1992, p. A21; Thomas B. Rosenstiel, "Candidates Meet Press Inquisition," *Los Angeles Times*, March 3, 1992, p. A1.

6. On the call-in phenomenon, see Thomas B. Rosenstiel, "The Talk Is about New Media," *Los Angeles Times*, May 23, 1992, p. A1; Elizabeth Kolbert, "Political Candidates and Call-In Shows: When the People Want to Be Heard,"

New York Times, June 10, 1992, p. A20; Thomas B. Rosenstiel, "Call-in Shows Question Tempo of Political Beat," *Los Angeles Times*, June 13, 1992, p. A1; Jonathan Alter, "How Phil Donahue Came to Manage the '92 Campaign," *Washington Monthly*, June 1992.

7. Quoted in Howard Kurtz, "Reports on Clinton Post Quandary for Journalists," *Washington Post*, January 30, 1992, p. A14.

8. Ward Just, "The Worst Political Coverage in My ... Memory," *Washington Post*, April 12, 1992, p. C7.

9. Anthony Lewis, "Hair on Their Chests," *New York Times*, April 19, 1992, sec. 4, p.11.

10. Quoted in Howard Kurtz, "Network TV Anchors Sharply Criticize Campaign Reporting," *Washington Post*, July 13, 1992, p. A11.

11. Vanocur's remarks were made at "Privacy in Politics: Has the Press Gone too Far?" Panel discussion sponsored by the Freedom Forum, July 13, 1992, New York.

12. Thomas Oliphant, "A Challenge to Journalism to Get Its Act Together," *Boston Globe*, June 7, 1992, p. 87.

13. See the poll of journalists in Times Mirror Center for the People and the Press, "The Campaign Press at Halftime," supplement to *Columbia Journalism Review*, July/August 1992.

14. Gail Collins, "Bearish on Bill/New York: Where the Fight Begins," *Newsday*, March 26, 1992, p. 6.

15. David S. Broder, "Democracy and the Press," *Washington Post*, January 3, 1990, p. A15.

16. For examples of bias criticism from the Left, see the issues of *Extra*, published by Fairness & Accuracy in Reporting (New York); and *Propaganda Review*, published by the Media Alliance (San Francisco); also see Martin A. Lee and Norman Solomon, *Unreliable Sources: A Guide to Detecting Bias in the News Media* (New York: Lyle Stuart, 1990). For bias criticism from the Right, see the issues of *AIM Report*, published by Accuracy in Media (Washington, D.C.); *Media Watch*, published by the Media Research Center (Alexandria, Va.); *Comint*, published by the Committee on Media Integrity (Hollywood, Calif.). On the phenomenon of media monitoring groups generally, see Dom Bonafede, "Taking on the Press," *National Journal*, April 8, 1989; Walter Goodman, "Let's Be Frank about Fairness and Accuracy," *New York Times*, June 17, 1990, sec. 2, p. 27.

17. On bias criticism playing into the hands of a complacent press, see Jay Rosen, "From Slogan to Spectacle: How the Media and the Left Lost the War," *Tikkun*, May/June 1991.

18. FAIR quote is from *Extra*, November/December 1990, p. 2; AIM quote is from a promotional pamphlet the organization sends in the mail; Comint quote is from Comint, Spring 1991, p. 7.

19. Vaclav Havel, *Living in Truth* (London: Faber & Faber, 1987).

20. Michael Sandel, *Liberalism and the Limits of Justice* (New York: Cambridge University Press, 1982), p. 183.

21. See Jay Rosen, "To Be or Not to Be? Newspapers May Be Our Last Hope for Recreating Public Life," *American Society of Newspaper Editors Bulletin*, October

1991; "Forming and Informing the Public," *Kettering Review*, Winter 1992; "Community Action: Sin or Salvation," *The Quill*, March 1992, from which this description is borrowed.

22. Personal interview with Watson, June 14, 1991. Jack Swift met an unfortunate death in 1990. Although Knight-Ridder had promoted his experiment as an exemplary case of community involvement, it did not insist that the experiment continue under the new editor, Al Johnson. The project, and particularly Swift's personal involvement as editor, met with criticism in the *Ledger-Enquirer* newsroom and remains controversial in the journalism profession. For reactions within the profession, see transcript of panel discussion, "Building Community Connections," Annual Conference of American Society of Newspaper Editors, Washington, D.C., April 8, 1992. On criticisms in the *Ledger-Enquirer* newsroom and the profession, see Jay Rosen, "The Press as a Political Actor: The Case of the Columbus (GA) *Ledger-Enquirer*," unpublished paper, 1990.

23. Knight-Ridder named Swift the winner of the company's Newspaper Customer Commitment Excellence Award and put him on the cover of its 1989 annual report. See also the remarks of the company's chairman, James K. Batten, "Newspapers and Communities: The Vital Link," Forty-first Annual William Allen White Speech, February 8, 1990 (Lawrence, Kan.: William Allen White Foundation, 1990).

24. Today, the inheritor of this cause within Knight-Ridder is Davis Merritt, Jr., and his colleagues at the *Wichita Eagle*, whose recent initiatives show some parallels to the Columbus experiment. See Stephen A. Smith, "Your Vote Counts: The *Wichita Eagle*'s Election Project," *National Civic Review*, Summer 1991, and Davis' remarks introducing the paper's "People Project," *Wichita Eagle*, June 21, 1992, p. 1A.

25. What Broder does not say is that media owners may, in their own way, oppose a more serious, public-minded press. The potential conflict between the journalists' agenda and the owners' agenda is an important and troublesome issue, but not my primary concern here. If it is true, as I've suggested, that journalists are in need of a new public philosophy, one of their bigger challenges is to convince owners that a press that supports public debate and civic participation is not hostile to ownership's interests.

26. David S. Broder, "Five Ways to Put Some Sanity Back in Elections," *Washington Post*, January 14, 1990, p. B1; on a similar theme, see Broder, "Hit the Streets: Find the Real Agenda," *The Quill*, March 1992. The most tangible result of Broder's urgings, and the experiment that comes closest to his election agenda for the press, is the *Charlotte Observer*'s revamped approach to campaign coverage, developed in partnership with the Poynter Institute for Media Studies. See editor Rich Oppel's announcement of the plan, *Charlotte Observer*, January 12, 1992, p. 9A; also see "The Charlotte Project: A Status Report," *Poynter Report* (St. Petersburg: Poynter Institute for Media Studies, Summer 1992), p. 11; Elizabeth Kolbert, "Paper Adjusts Reporting by Asking Its Readers," *New York Times*, June 21, 1992, Sec. 1, p. 20.

27. Quoted in Paul Taylor, *See How They Run: Electing Presidents in an Age of Mediaocracy* (New York: Knopf, 1990), p. 6.

28. All quotations are from the transcript of "Donahue," April 1, 1992 (New York: Multimedia Entertainment, 1992). Melissa Roth was identified in Douglas Jehl, "Clinton Takes a Grilling in N.Y. and Gains an Audience," *Los Angeles Times*, April 2, 1992, p. A12.

29. A classic text for this view is the Hutchins Commission report. Robert Leigh, ed., *A Free and Responsible Press: Report of the Commission on Freedom of the Press* (Chicago: Midway Reprint, 1974).

30. Lee C. Bollinger, *Images of a Free Press* (Chicago: University of Chicago Press, 1991), pp. 72–73. The *Red Lion* decision is *Red Lion Broadcasting Co. v. Federal Communications Commission*, 395 U.S. 367 (1969).

31. See David S. Broder, "Running Scared," *Washington Post*, June 24, 1992, p. A19.

32. On campaign technology, see Dan Balz, "Candidates Skirt News Media, Favor Direct Delivery of Message," *Washington Post*, May 19, 1992, p. A1.

33. In addition to Broder, see Michael Kinsley, "Ask a Silly Question," *The New Republic*, July 6, 1992, p. 6; Richard Harwood, "Media Wilt: The Waning Power of the Press," *Washington Post*, June 26, 1992, p. A23; Jonathan Alter, "How Phil Donahue Came to Manage the '92 Campaign," *Washington Monthly*, June 1992; and Paul Taylor's companion piece in this volume.

34. In July 1991, executives from seventeen leading news organizations sent a report to Secretary of Defense Dick Cheney protesting restrictions on reporters during the war. See Jason DeParle, "17 News Executives Criticize U.S. For 'Censorship' of Gulf Coverage," *New York Times*, July 3, 1991, p. A4. See also Jason DeParle, "Keeping the News in Step: Are the Pentagon's Gulf War Rules Here to Stay?" *New York Times*, May 6, 1991, p. A9. For comments on the restrictions from a wide range of journalists, see "The Media and the Gulf: A Closer Look," conference proceedings, May 3–4, 1991, Graduate School of Journalism, University of California, Berkeley.

35. During the war, a survey by the Times Mirror Center for the People and the Press found that almost 80 percent of Americans supported the Pentagon's restrictions on journalists, with almost 60 percent in favor of greater controls. See Howard Kurtz, "Media's Mixed Reviews: Public Favors Pentagon Limits on War Coverage," *Washington Post*, January 31, 1991, p. C2.

36. Jason DeParle, "Keeping the News in Step: Are the Pentagon's Gulf War Rules Here to Stay?" *New York Times*, May 6, 1991, p. A9. See also Jason DeParle, "Long Series of Military Decisions Led to Gulf War News Censorship," *New York Times*, May 5, 1991, p. A1.

37. See, for example, Stanley W. Cloud, "Covering the Next War," *New York Times*, August 4, 1992, p. A19.

38. Henry Allen, "The Gulf Between the Media and the Military: In Briefing Room Skirmishes, the Officers Score a Lopsided Victory," *Washington Post*, February 21, 1991, p. D1.

39. This analysis is borrowed from Jay Rosen, "Cynicism Works—If You're Bogart," *Los Angeles Times*, May 30, 1991, p. A21.

40. Daniel Yankelovich, *Coming to Public Judgment: Making Democracy Work in a Complex World* (Syracuse: Syracuse University Press, 1991, pp. 5–6.

41. Ibid., pp. 24–31, 59–60.

42. Christopher Lasch, "Journalism, Publicity and the Lost Art of Argument," *Gannett Center Journal*, Spring 1990, p. 1. On this theme, see also Jay Rosen, "No Content: The Press, Politics and Public Philosophy," *Tikkun*, May/June, 1992.

43. Christopher Lasch, "Academic Pseudo-Radicalism: The Charade of 'Subversion,'" *Salmagundi*, nos. 88–89, Fall 1990-Winter 1991, p. 32.

44. Randolph Ryan, "Clinton Stands Tall," *Boston Globe*, February 15, 1992, p. 13.

Political Coverage in the 1990s:
Teaching the Old News New Tricks

by Paul Taylor

W hen did the change happen? Was it when Ross Perot solicited his own draft on "Larry King Live"? When Bill Clinton stumped for votes on MTV? When Jerry Brown shilled his 800 number on a nationally televised debate? When Gennifer Flowers sold her story to the *Star*? When Vice Presidential Press Secretary David C. Beckwith identified himself only as "Dave from DC" as he phoned in a defense of his boss during one of the radio talk-show bashings to which Quayle is regularly subjected? Or was it when Presidential Press Secretary Marlin Fitzwater allowed that even *his* boss might have to hit television's gabfest circuit, but put "The Arsenio Hall Show"—where Clinton had donned some cheap shades and blew his saxophone a week earlier—off-limits? (In Arsenio's neighborhood, one good "dis" begets another, and here's how one of the high priests of the New Media Order returned fire in his monologue that mid-June night: "Excuse me, George Herbert irregular-heart-beating, read-my-lipping, slipping-in-the-polls, do-nothing, deficit-raising, make-less-money-than-Millie-the-White-House-dog-last-year, Quayle-loving, sushi-puking Bush! I don't remember inviting your ass to my show.")

The change came in all of these moments, and dozens more like them in the astonishing spring of 1992. Running for president in Talk-Show America turns out to be a bit messier than running for president in a world where the network news shows pretty much hosted the whole affair, and saw to it that people minded their manners. It's ruder, it's cruder, it's sometimes lewder, but on balance, it's almost certainly better for democracy.

The "almost" belongs in the previous sentence because the phenomenon is so new that it's still wrapped in caveats. Will the New Media Order prove to be a passing fancy or a permanent realignment? Will ratings for political fare remain high in nontraditional forums—as they were throughout the spring and summer of 1992—or will the American public's notoriously short attention span find other diversions by the time this election day rolls around, or the next, or the one after that? And, by the way, if Talk-Show America is bringing so many new listeners, viewers, and readers into the public square, why did voter turnout fall in the 1992 Democratic primaries by 16 percent over 1988?[1] (Part of the reason was that the talk-show phenomena didn't kick into high gear until after the New York primary, by which time Clinton had clinched the nomination, depressing turnout in the later primaries. But part of it also was that voter turnout in this country has been on a steady and steep decline for the past 32 years.)

Finally—and for the purposes of this paper, most critically—how will the journalistic standards of the New News (as it's been dubbed by *Rolling Stone* magazine) affect the standards of the Old News? Are we doomed, when a Gennifer Flowers bounds across the political firmament, to have her newsworthiness fixed by the *Star* rather than by the *New York Times*; by Geraldo, Phil, and Oprah instead of Peter, Tom, and Dan? Are we fated to have the lowest common denominator always be the operative formula for news judgment during the political season? Must the Old News meet the challenge of the New News by becoming more like it?

Or might it be possible for the Old News to adopt some of the New News's healthiest innovations—such as long interviews, easy access, and lots of unmediated communication between voters and candidates—while maintaining standards that constrain the New News's coarser instincts, such as a fixation on the trivial, the personal, the angry, the weird? In short, must all norms in this rapidly changing media environment bubble up from below, or might some simultaneously trickle down from above?

This paper will argue that it is both possible and desirable for the elite media to behave like an elite, and it will offer suggestions on how they should redefine their mission and retool their practices to best play that role. Some of the changes to be advocated here can be implemented within the craft, and some will have to be imposed from without by a modest degree of regulation. All are designed to induce elite political journalists to define their role not simply as one of telling stories, but as raising the level of public discourse—or, as Jay Rosen puts it in the companion paper in this volume, as "improving the manner in which the political community converses with itself."

"Elite" is an unfashionable word in a political era in which middle-class populism is on the loose, but it's a useful concept for a democratic society whose political cues seem to come more and more from an all-powerful, ever-changing, commercially driven popular culture. Without standards for political discourse set by elites and shaped by something other than the marketplace, the public square might become noisier and more animated in Talk-Show America, but what happens there will only deepen the public cynicism that has led to gridlock in the halls of government and a profound sense of disconnectedness from public life everywhere else.

To be clear from the outset, the argument here isn't that the elite media have been doing such a terrific job that they can't stand improvement. To the contrary, the bad habits of the Old News have contributed to today's raging popular frustration both with public life and with the reporting of it. The New News owes much of its existence to the arteriosclerosis of the Old News. And while there is nothing like fresh competition to shake up a troubled institution ("pooped, confused and broke" is the way the *Rolling Stone* piece described the Old News),[2] it's not yet clear whether the inevitable shakeout will be for the better or the worse.

By the term "Old News" I mean to describe the network news shows, the Sunday morning interview and commentary shows, the weekly news magazines, and the prestige national and regional newspapers whose collective news judgments form the closest thing the journalistic establishment has to a code of standard practices.

Old News's bad habits in the field of political and governmental reporting can be grouped into four categories. One is the tendency to sensationalize and trivialize public life, to turn elections into contests of personalities and tactics rather than ideas and proposals, and to measure these personalities with criteria that titillate more than illuminate. Is it any wonder, once the coverage of two consecutive presidential campaigns has wallowed for a spell in the bedrooms of the leading candidates, that Phil Donahue and his kind will want to elbow in on the action?

Another bad habit is the tendency to look for the wart or the easy exposé; to conduct this search in a jaded voice that encourages viewers, listeners, and readers to believe the worst about politicians and public life and that robs the public square of the dignity it deserves. This corrosive, bad-news bias in political coverage can be as subtle as the "smart-aleck" close that so many network political correspondents use at the end of so many ninety-second political pieces. Or it can be as frontal as the whole media establishment deciding in early 1992 (after a jump start by radio talk shows) that the mismanagement of the House of Representatives Bank constituted a major scandal. They decided this despite the fact that the lax practices of that disbursement office had been in effect for a century and a half, that overdrafts were more common a generation ago than they had been in recent years, and that no taxpayer money was ever lost because of the sloppy bookkeeping.

The emergence of a New News will only amplify these two bad habits. By New News I mean the hodgepodge that covers everything from Jay

Leno's monologue to Larry King's talk show to David Letterman's top
ten list, from rap music to talk radio to public affairs programming on
cable, from Spike Lee to Bart Simpson to Public Enemy, from tabloid
television to MTV to C-SPAN, from "infotainment" shows to long-format interviews to call-in shows that aspire to create a plebiscitary
rather than a representative democracy—in other words, a mix of the
serious, the slightly bizarre and the au courant; in other words, the "everywhere" culture.

The New News, even more than the old, feasts on political stories that
come packaged as morality plays, soap operas, or "gotcha" cat-and-mouse
games. The more trivial, the more simple-minded, the more trashy, the
more cynical, the better. Its sense of mission is built almost entirely around
staying in sync with the regnant populist outrage. Unlike the Old News,
it doesn't fail to maintain standards of balance, nuance, perspective;
it never aspired to these standards in the first place. Veteran journalist
Carl Bernstein of Watergate fame, in a piece in *The New Republic* entitled
"The Idiot Culture," observed:

> For more than fifteen years we have been moving away from
> real journalism toward the creation of a sleazoid info-tainment
> culture in which the lines between Oprah and Phil and
> Geraldo and Diane and even Ted, between the New York
> *Post* and *Newsday*, are too often indistinguishable. In this
> new culture of journalistic titillation, we teach our readers and
> viewers that the trivial is significant, that the lurid and the loopy
> are more important than the real news. We do not serve our
> readers and viewers, we pander to them. And we conde-
> scend to them, giving them what we think they want and
> what we calculate will sell and boost ratings and readership.
> Many of them, sadly, seem to justify our condescension, and
> to kindle at the trash. Still, it is the role of journalists to chal-
> lenge people, not merely to amuse them.[3]

If the New News had only this sleazy side, Bernstein's screed would
be on target. But the New News, at least as I have chosen to define it,
is a hydra-headed beast. Some of it is loopy, some deadly serious.
Remember, it runs the gamut from "Entertainment Tonight" to C-
Span. And its substantive side holds out promise as an antidote to the
other two bad habits of the Old News.

One is that the Old News has become a discourteous host of the
presidential extravaganza, forever stealing the spotlight from its presumed guests of honor. The famous statistic goes like this: In 1968 the

average sound bite (a segment of uninterrupted speech) for a presidential candidate lasted 42 seconds on the network evening news shows. By 1988, it was down to 9.8 seconds,[4] and in the first five months of the 1992 campaign it fell to 7.3 seconds, according to the Center for Media and Public Affairs (CMPA), a watchdog group based in Washington, D.C.

The less time the network news correspondents were giving the candidates, the more they were hogging for themselves. A CMPA survey in June 1992 found that reporters' comments took up 72 percent of all election news airtime on the network evening news shows in 1992, while quotes from voters, political experts, and other sources made up 15 percent and sound bites from the candidates made up just 13 percent. Daniel C. Hallin, an associate professor of communication at the University of California, San Diego, using a slightly different yardstick, has found that sound bites filled up only 5.7 percent of the 1988 election coverage on television, down from 17.6 percent in 1968.[5] "What these figures show is that the message is getting more and more mediated," said S. Robert Lichter, codirector of the CMPA. "The candidates can only get snippets on the air, and it is frustrating to them and to the electorate."[6]

To fill the vacuum, along comes the New News, with its call-in shows, its two-hour-long candidate interviews, its direct-access electronic fundraising, its promise of turning the campaign into a giant conference call. This transformation was clearly of a piece with the emergence in the early spring of 1992 of H. Ross Perot, the plain-talking, self-made, bantam-weight populist billionaire from Texarkana, as potentially the most serious independent candidate since Teddy Roosevelt ran as a Bull Moose in 1912. In the dizzying weeks and months of his takeoff, Perot masterfully sidestepped the media establishment and helped to give birth to a new kind of easy-access political television. He eschewed press conferences and press planes, he played on the public's resentment of the junkyard dog demeanor of the political press, and he limited his appearances to comfortable chats with the likes of Larry King, David Frost, and Katie Couric.

Not only that, but the populist billionaire's most daring proposal was to conduct his presidency as a kind of episodic electronic town hall, with his administration's policies shaped by the wisdom he would glean from his periodic exchanges with viewers and listeners. Never mind that the last thing America's adrift political system seems to need at this moment is more pandering to an angry middle class. As journalist Nicholas Lemann has written, politicians have been paying attention to the middle class with "fantastic devotion" for the past dozen years;[7] witness the piling up of $3 trillion of debt, which represents nothing more or less than the refusal of elected officials to ask the people who elected them to pony up and pay for the goods and services that government provides and that they demand.

Perot will never get the chance to put his vision of a plebiscitary democracy into practice; his devotion to the will of the people turned out to be a tad more shallow than advertised. At the first sign of trouble on the political trail, he took a hike. But the see-me, feel-me, touch-me ambience of campaign coverage he helped to inspire could well turn out to be the most lasting contribution of his candidacy. Some of this might have happened without him; the change in the ambience of coverage predated and to some extent anticipated his brief sojourn as a politician. In the critical showdown battle for the Democratic presidential nomination—the bare-knuckled New York primary—the masters of ceremony turned out to be two leading New News figures, television's Phil Donahue and radio's Don Imus. Clinton probably went further in New York than anywhere else to put to rest the incessant questioning about his extramarital life when—to the delight of the studio audience—he threatened that he would clam up if Donahue didn't stop asking questions about Gennifer Flowers. Clinton had an equally successful exchange (this time his weapon was self-deprecating humor) with his nemesis on New York talk radio, WFAN's Don Imus.

But it's a mistake to infer from these two examples that these non-traditional forums are always a cakewalk for the politicians. Talk radio hasn't doubled in listenership since 1985 because the deejays are out to make nice with the politicians. The 1990 congressional pay raise was killed by radio talk-show hosts, and the 1992 House Bank scandal story was overblown by the elite media in part because they proved to be such a blood-boiler in the hands of the gadflies of talk radio.

It's also wrong to leave the impression that the only important changes in the format of political coverage in 1992 came on these nontraditional venues. As soon as Donahue and King showed that there was a market for long political interviews, the network morning news shows moved in. And they, too, discovered a market. When Perot answered questions for two hours on the "Today" Show on June 11 (the show's longest such interview in NBC producers' memories), the show drew a 4.9 Nielsen rating for its first hour and a 5.3 for its second—well above its 3.8 average, and tying the high ratings of coverage of the L.A. riots and the Persian Gulf War. (Each rating point represents 921,000 homes.)

Longer format political coverage doesn't always have such political pull. Clinton, appearing the same week, drew a 3.2 rating. Clinton also bought a half hour of prime time on NBC the night of June 12, in the 8:00–8:30 p.m. time slot, to answer questions from a studio audience.

It drew a 4.5 national rating, well below the 6.4 rating of an NBC news special on guns in the same slot the week before. A month later, on the opening night of the Democratic National Convention, the three major networks drew just 30 percent of all viewers, two percentage points fewer than watched the 1988 opening night, and eleven points below the 1984 opener. Fox Television's feature film the first night of the 1992 convention, *The Revenge of the Nerds, Part III,* drew significantly more viewers than the first half-hour's coverage by CBS, NBC, and ABC, all of which had scaled back their televised coverage of the convention either to an hour or ninety minutes a night (though on several nights the actual coverage ran over the allotted time). For the rest of the convention week, viewership on the networks of the 1992 Democratic convention continued to be below 1988, which was below 1984. The Republicans, if anything, fared even worse. As this mixed bag suggests, there was a predictably low ceiling of viewer interest in substantive fare, especially once Perot dropped out.

Meantime, as new outlets continued to open up, the already ragged line between news and entertainment continued to blur. After the Democratic convention was over each night, Tom Brokaw did a brief comedy turn on the "Tonight" show, trading jokes with Jay Leno about the evening's events. Cable's Comedy Channel called its coverage of both conventions "Indecision '92," and MTV did snippets of convention coverage between its music videos. Even Bart Simpson got into the act while "watching" a rerun of the Republican convention. When real-life President Bush pleaded for an America that looked more "like the Waltons and a lot less like the Simpsons," the cartoon character snapped back, "We're just like the Waltons. We're praying for the depression to end, too."

The best part of this let-a-thousand-flowers-bloom spring and summer of politics on television was that it gave candidates chances to get their message out, free and clear. By mid-June there were so many television hosts offering so many long interviews and call-in formats that the Clinton campaign canceled plans for a second half hour of paid time. "If you gave me $3 million today, I wouldn't spend a penny on TV. We can't get any more [exposure] than we are getting," explained Deputy Campaign Manager George Stephanopoulos.[8] Business was so brisk that the *New York Times,* the *Washington Post,* and other elite papers began running daily "Candidates on Television" boxes on their political pages, alerting their readers which channel to flip to for their daily fix.

And it wasn't just John Q. Public who was leaping at the chance to phone in questions to the men who would be president. In late June, when Republican National Committee Chairman Richard Bond wanted to try to take Perot down a peg, he chose to do so as the first caller to CNN's

"Larry King Live," which had Perot on as a guest. (Great moment in television, circa 1992: King: "I guess you know Ross." Bond: "I do. Hey, Mr. Perot." Perot: "Have we ever met?"). The more this kind of thing went on, the more barriers came down. Even MTV ran a "Choose or Lose" special with Clinton that ranged from a discussion of his early rock influences ("Going nuts over Elvis") to his sign (Leo) to his revelation of his preferred Supreme Court Justice candidate (Mario Cuomo).

"I think it's terrific," said Stephen Hess, a senior fellow at the Brookings Institution who specializes in the study of the media:

> Any time you expose more people to the men and women who run our government, or aspire to run it, it's a good thing. This doesn't mean I want the *Washington Post* or the networks to close up shop. But these new formats are complementary. MTV and Donahue reach people who don't read newspapers or watch the network news. Maybe the candidates aren't being asked hardball questions that political reporters ask, but we are learning some things.

Lichter, of the CMPA, saw the emergence of these formats as a new theater of combat in the continuing warfare between the candidates and the establishment media over who controls the news agenda. "If you're running for president, you'd prefer talking to Katie Couric than to Lesley Stahl, and to anyone in the phone book over Sam Donaldson," he observed:

> In 1988, we saw presidential candidates getting around the network anchors and political correspondents by discovering the world of local television. This year, they are finding these alternate forums like Donahue and Larry King and the "Today Show." It's all part of the ongoing struggle between journalists and candidates. Candidates are always trying to force coverage into their most comfortable venue, whether that means adopting a Rose Garden strategy or setting up a photo op in a flag factory, or buying commercial time to get their unmediated message out. What we're seeing this year is another expansion of the options available to them. I don't think that's at all bad. We still have the nightly news to tell us what is serious and what isn't. It still functions as a legitimizer of news.

It's worth pointing out that for all the huffing and puffing, these call-in shows are a field of dreams for the candidates, filled with softball questions; the New News shows gave the Old News pros a run for their money. The night after Perot's surprise withdrawal from the race, it was Larry King who had the Texan on live in his studio and who gave disappointed campaign workers a chance to vent their frustration and ask their candidate (who was clearly discomfitted) why he'd abandoned them. At the exact same time, "20/20" ran a rather tired interview, taped earlier that day, in which Barbara Walters lobbed questions that the ex-candidate handled with much more aplomb. Or consider a little exercise that Michael Kinsley of *The New Republic* conducted in the midst of the format explosion. After acknowledging that there is "something eerie about the same show discussing men-who-would-be-president one day and women-who-ate-their-husbands the next," Kinsley compared the first ten questions asked of President Bush by the White House press corps at his June 4 press conference with the first ten asked of Perot by viewers when he appeared on "Today" a week later in a call-in format. "The most striking difference . . . is that the pros are obsessed with process while the amateurs are obsessed with substance," Kinsley noted.[9] Here, condensed, are the first five questions put to Bush by the pros:

1. Will you debate Ross Perot in the fall campaign?
2. Is it proper for a man like Perot to use his wealth to run for president, and is Perot an insider or an outsider?
3. Do the opinion polls reflect a rejection of your message?
4. Do you agree with Dan Quayle that Perot was wrong in opposing the Gulf War?
5. If you are reelected, will you submit a balanced budget in 1994?

Here are the first five put by the amateurs to Perot:

1. When will you officially declare your candidacy?
2. Are you pro-choice or pro-life?
3. What would you do as president to put unemployed Americans back to work?
4. What are your views on farm policy, especially concerning dairy farms?
5. Would you raise taxes to balance the budget?

The fixation of the White House press corps on process goes to the fourth and last bad habit of the Old News—its tendency to construct political campaigns as a game of inside baseball, with its own arcane rules and strategies, clever ploys and dirty tricks, all of which are of endless fascination to the players and commentators but have precious little to do with safe streets, decent jobs, or enough money to put the kids through college. "Journalists and presidential aspirants have become textbook co-dependents," Jon Katz wrote in *Rolling Stone*, "hooked on one another for status and survival. . . . The rest of the world is always outside, too dumb to understand, too powerless to be paid attention to, too removed to get the lingo or understand the rules or the significance."[10] Hallin has found that ordinary voters were featured in 20 percent of the network news sound bites in 1972 and 1976 but claimed only 3 and 4 percent in 1984 and 1988. "Voters now appear in the news essentially to illustrate poll results and almost never to contribute ideas or arguments to campaign coverage," Hallin wrote in a piece that appeared just before the emergence of the new formats. "Here again the position of TV news is ironic. Just as TV folks decry 'photo opportunity' and 'sound bite' campaigning even while building the news around them, so they decry the vision of the campaign consultant, with its emphasis on technique over substance, while adopting that culture as their own."[11]

This plague of insiderism is one of the reasons the public got so fed up with the Old News. In a nationwide poll conducted by the Gordon S. Black Corporation in 1992, 70 percent of those surveyed agreed that "so-called experts on national television don't understand the things that concern me"; 73 percent agreed that the "national networks have gotten way out of touch with what most Americans really think"; and 89 percent agreed that "newspapers would rather take cheap shots at candidates' personal lives than help voters understand issues."[12] The Old News, in short, has become a carrier as well as a chronicler of the prevailing discontent with public life.

Given the distemper of its viewers and readers, and given the competition it now faces from a whole new format of news, how should the Old News mend its ways? This question, in one form or another, gets tossed around after every campaign by an increasingly self-conscious Old News establishment. The presidential cycle for political journalists nowadays seems to run a full four years—two for actually covering the campaign, two more for engaging in rituals of self-flagellation at symposiums held at the finest universities around the country. The sessions that followed the 1988 campaign were especially brutal, but there was a difference. A concrete reform was actually put in practice during the midterm campaigns of 1990. Unfortunately, it's an example of a change that contributes as much to the problem as the solution. And it illustrates a larger conundrum for Old News journalists: often with the best of intentions, they continue to define their mission in a way that isn't likely to raise the level of the political discourse. Before there can be effective reform, the Old News needs to rethink its mission.

The reform was the creation of "Ad Watch" features, both in newspapers and on some television stations, designed to expose the deceit or innuendo or half-truths in political ads on television. There is no disputing the journalistic rationale for such features. In the decade of the 1980s, thirty-second political ads on television became nastier and more numerous than ever before. They obviously cried out to be subjected to the same standards of independent scrutiny as a candidate's speech, press conference, position paper, or biography. The failure of journalists to provide such scrutiny in the past derived in part from a mechanical problem: the most effective attack ads are extraverbal and nonlinear, and traffic in false impressions rather than outright falsehoods, leaving print journalists, in particular, without a readily accessible language to take them on. It also derived from a source problem: the cozy relationship that has grown up between the consultants who make the ads and the reporters who cover the campaigns (see Katz, above) has often left journalists inclined to pull their punches. As Rosen notes, the *Washington Post*'s David Broder blew the whistle on this journalistic dereliction in an influential essay he wrote at the start of the 1990 campaign. It urged journalists around the country to take up the fight against deceitful political advertising on television. Scores of newspapers and television stations rallied to the cause. I was the reporter at the *Post* who inaugurated the newspaper's ad watch feature in early 1990— a format that consisted of a photograph of one or more frames of a political ad, the script of the ad, and commentary supplied either by the reporter or some neutral third party to highlight any false impressions being created by the words, the images, or the juxtaposition of the two.

But in the spirit of journalistic self-flagellation, a confession: I felt ambivalent then, and feel ambivalent now, about these ad watch boxes. As University of Virginia assistant professor of rhetoric Michael Cornfield has observed, they are "twice removed from political reality."[13] And as Hallin has written, they help give coverage of campaigns "a kind of knowing, postmodern cynicism that debunks the image and the image-maker and yet in the end seems to accept them as the only reality citizens have left."[14] The writer Louis Menand made a similar point in *The New Republic* in 1989. It wasn't about ad watches, but it might as well have been:

> One often heard the complaint in the 80s that the press was manipulated by images. But the press reported on manipulation night and day. Fakery was a virtual journalistic theme

in the last two presidential campaigns. The point is how little [the reporting] mattered. Americans know perfectly well
that everything is packaged; the packaging comes, in effect,
already discredited. . . . The acceptance of a disparity between
thought and conduct, between image and reality has become
a mark of our sophistication.[15]

Exposing fakery is a time-honored role for journalism; there's no
suggestion here that ad watches be discontinued. Rather, the proposition is that the search for improvements in journalism has to go in other,
more positive directions if the nation is to break free of its terrible
despair about public life. For quite some time now, the public square
has been more like a vicious circle. The fakery of the candidates
(whether through attack ads or through empty promises, on the order
of "Read my lips: no new taxes") begets the cynicism of the reporters
and voters, and the cynicism of the reporters and voters begets fakery
and attack politics, because these tactics work best when the public is
poised to believe the worst about the candidates. Around and around
it has gone, with voter frustration rising and turnout falling, with government gridlock growing because no politician ever seems to get
elected with an affirmative mandate to do anything—and because
every politician is so cowed by the populist anger, the whole system is
stuck in a defensive crouch.

What can journalism do to improve things? Its role in the scheme of
things is limited, but it does have a role. With the decline of political
parties, journalists have increasingly become players in a political
contest in which they also serve as observers, commentators, and
referees. Political stories don't just "happen" the way hailstorms do.
They are artifacts of a political universe that journalism itself has
helped to construct. They are components of a journalistic master narrative built around two principal story lines: the search for candidates' character flaws, and the depiction of the campaign as a
horserace, full of ploys and surprises, tenacity and treachery, rising action
and falling action, winners and losers.

But as Rosen has argued elsewhere, *elections* are about winning;
campaigns should offer the public a context for their votes. What the
journalist must do, he writes, paraphrasing Christopher Lasch, is to:

construct the political universe in such a way that the activity that is most visible is discussion and debate. Politics
becomes an arena for public talk, and this talk should be
productive in the sense that it permits us to see the political

sphere as meaningful—connected to our lives, conducted in a language we share, incomplete without our participation.[16]

This, then, ought to be the new mission of the Old News political journalist: not simply to tell stories carved out of a master narrative that reflects many of journalism's bad habits, but to improve the political discourse. By my lights, the conversation of politics nourishes precisely to the degree that it defines public life as something larger than the sum of private interests. A nation without a substantive public discourse lacks the glue to bind the hopes and fears of its citizens into a sense of common purpose. As philosopher Michael Sandel has put it: "When politics goes well we can know a good that we cannot know alone."[17] Our political talk, in other words, ought to serve as a bridge. At the moment, it is a wedge.

How should journalistic practices change in order to achieve this mission? The craft's list of self-improvement vows is long, familiar, and mostly honored in the breach: more attention to issues, less to the horserace, fewer photo ops, longer sound bites, and so on. In early July 1992, CBS Evening News—embarrassed by reports from watchdog groups that after all the fuss over shrinking sound bites in 1988, the little critters got *even smaller* in the 1992 primary season—adopted an experimental policy of only running sound bites from presidential candidates that lasted at least thirty seconds. "There is a lot of mixed opinion on our staff about this," Executive Producer Erik Sorenson said in announcing the change, "but there is at least some validity to the criticism that you don't get to hear the candidates air it out on the evening newscasts."[18] The policy is certainly a welcome step, but as soon as it was implemented, a potentially troublesome side effect cropped up: to comply with their own rules, CBS executives said they had thrown out some candidate sound bites altogether in the first week, either because they were too short or were deemed to be too unwieldy to be placed in the middle of a political piece. Meantime, news executives at NBC and ABC said they would never institute such a rule, calling it inflexible and arbitrary. On a more promising note, all three major networks were offering segments of the stump speeches, as well as in-depth reports on issues and on the backgrounds of the candidates—meaty if conventional fare.

But the most troublesome bad habit of political journalism isn't the shrinking sound bite; it's the indiscriminate way the media probe for the warts of the men who would be president. This is where the Old Media most need to redefine their mission and clean up their act. Here, the challenge isn't so much to construct new standards on such tricky issues as the presumption of privacy, the relevance of personal life, the need for balance and the reporting of rumors about public officials. It is to revive some old standards mistakenly presumed dead in a society where everyone seems to know everything about the private lives of public figures. And it is to have the courage to hold the line on these standards, even knowing that most of the New News competitors won't.

"Sometimes I think you folks [in the media] are in the business of [finding] the darkest moment of the darkest hour of the darkest week of the darkest year in anyone's life," Bill Clinton lamented after his trial-by-media ordeal over allegations of marital infidelity was followed by another over allegations of draft evasion, and another over his belated confession that he had smoked pot as a college student (but never inhaled).[19] He blamed the media for what he called the "wall of cynicism" that politicians confront every time they face voters, a wall that makes honest dialogue next to impossible. Leave aside a moment the self-evident truth that the politicians bring much of the cynicism on themselves. Let's also stipulate that Clinton has a point. "Those of us who practice journalism must ask . . . whether we too are contributing to this [voter] distemper by our relentless assaults on every crack and flaw in a candidate's past and our willful refusal to explore any shine in the armor," David Gergen, editor at large of *U.S. News & World Report*, wrote in the July 6 issue. Content analyses of television coverage of the past several presidential campaigns has shown that the "spin" supplied by the reporters and by supposedly neutral sources has been consistently negative; in 1988, for example, the ratio of coverage on the network news programs was two-to-one negative over positive for both Bush and Dukakis, according to the Center for Media and Public Affairs.

This is not all bad. Exposing the hidden flaws, ripping the bark off everyone and everything that wields power, bringing the high and mighty to account—these are the instincts at the heart of the best kind of anti-institutional, reform-minded, populist journalism. "A journalist is the lookout on the bridge of the ship of state," Joseph Pulitzer wrote in 1904. "He peers through fog and storm to give warning of dangers ahead . . . . He is there to watch over the safety and the welfare of the people who trust him."[20] Mix that keen sense of civic guardianship with the decline of political parties as screening committees for presidential candidates, and who else is there to stand guard at the White House gate, fending off the shallow, the reckless, the disingenuous? Americans do not elect position papers to high office; they elect human beings—and they must know who the candidates are, what they are made of, where they have been, what they believe. Who will tell them, if not the media?

But no matter how vital this role, it begs a couple of equally vital questions. When does the journalist cross the line between healthy skep-

ticism and corrosive cynicism? How can our society expect a better breed
of politician if its journalists convey such a low opinion of political life?
And lastly, how does the "lookout" keep from becoming a voyeur?

No question has given journalists more fits in the past two presidential
campaigns than that last one: whether to report the sexual peccadilloes
of candidates. In 1987, front-running Gary Hart dropped out of the presidential campaign six days after the *Miami Herald* revealed—as a result
of a surveillance that its reporters conducted in response to an anony-
mous tip—that Hart had just spent the weekend in his Washington town-
house with a Miami model, Donna Rice.[21] In early 1992, Bill Clinton's
candidacy seemed to teeter on the brink when Gennifer Flowers, a
sometime cabaret singer/sometime state employee from Arkansas,
sold the story of her alleged twelve-year affair with Clinton to the *Star*
for a reported six-figure sum.

One reason these stories create such a stir within the craft of journalism
is that our society has no commonly accepted standard about when,
if ever, a candidate's marital and sexual life is relevant to his or her qual-
ifications for public office. Some take the view that cheating on one's
spouse says something important about one's private morality, which
in turn says something important about one's public morality—evok-
ing the old refrain from the 1960s that the personal is political. Some
say the cheating isn't the issue, but lying about it can be. Some say it's
not the cheating or the lying, but the recklessness, the promiscuity, the
lack of judgment. By this standard, a discreet affair is different from a
string of one-night stands. Some argue that private and public character
traits are different kettles of fish: we sometimes want our leaders to be
cold and ruthless; we always want our friends to be warm and empath-
ic. Some argue that, given this wide range of opinions and perspectives,
the most useful thing journalism can do is to report the private lives of
public figures as fully and fairly as possible, then let each reader,
viewer, and voter sort it all out. This is the cult of Know-Everythingism.
But others argue that the most useful thing journalism can do under
the circumstances is to ignore the subject altogether, knowing that
when stories about sex come along, subtlety, nuance, and balance will
get chucked out the window, and all other matters of greater relevance will get crowded out of the public square. This the cult of Know-
Nothingism.

It would be a lot tidier if either of the absolutist standards were real-
istic, but, alas, they're not. Know-Nothingism? Suppose a candidate likes
to spend his recreational time looking at pictures of nudes? Shouldn't
the public be alerted? Know-Everythingism? Suppose a candidate has
had an abortion, a matter she very much wants to keep private? Must

the public be told? Suppose she's spent her political career opposing abortion? Does that affect the calculation?

There are no easy answers—and even if there were, journalism would resist codifying them into a set of standards. Journalism is a craft, not a profession. It prefers ad hockery to standards, in part out of a healthy fear that fixed rules are an invitation to an unhealthy uniformity— and to self-censorship. What it does have are a set of shared instincts, which reflect (and, in turn, help to shape) the mores, tastes, and values of the society it reports. These instincts change as society changes. A half century ago, in an era more respectful of privacy, President Franklin D. Roosevelt was confined to a wheelchair and could be assured that the press would engage in a benign conspiracy never to let his constituents know about it. He could also have his train take a detour on its runs between Washington and Hyde Park for stops on a New Jersey siding for a rendezvous with Lucy Mercer Rutherford, secure in the knowledge that the reporters traveling with him would never publish a word. Then, along came television, with its extraordinary power to bring politicians into our living rooms every night. Naturally the public's curiosity about who they really were, with the bark off, ratcheted up several notches. It is beside the point whether this change has been for the better or the worse. One cannot uninvent television. One cannot repeal *People* magazine. Nor can one wish away the simple truth that as technology has made our culture more media-soaked, the way we measure political leaders has become more personality-soaked— and the zone of privacy that politicians once enjoyed has shrunk.

President Kennedy was the first politician in the modern era (but certainly not the last) to realize that these changes could offer benefits to someone in public life. He invited the camera in to record the private moments of his enormously attractive family, and by so doing conjured up a latter-day Camelot. We now know there were different kinds of private moments that Kennedy enjoyed when the cameras were pointed the other way. In this regard, he was a transitional figure—taking advantage of the media's new intrusiveness, but paying none of the penalties, not even when his taste in mistresses took him recklessly into the arms of a mobster moll named Judith Exner.

Nowadays, the media no longer avert their gaze. They take the position that if public figures maneuver the new intrusiveness to their advantage, they also should be prepared to withstand scrutiny that may put them in a less shining light. If Bill Clinton wants to tell the story, as a parable about his character, of the time he stood up to his alcoholic stepfather and told him to stop beating his mother, he is inviting all of the media some of the way into his zone of privacy. Ditto for Al

Gore when he talks movingly on the campaign trail about coming to a fuller emotional understanding of himself after his son was nearly killed in an automobile accident. The proposition here is that politicians themselves have something to do with setting the boundaries of their zone of privacy.

This isn't a hard and fast rule (Gary Hart tried zealously to guard his privacy; all he got for his trouble was a media corps more persuaded than ever that he was something of a social misfit). But it's one good place to draw an admittedly fuzzy line: the more a candidate talks about his or her private life, the more it becomes fair game. Are there other rough rules for the elite media to follow? Once we have agreed it is impossible to ignore private lives, just as it is irresponsible to fixate on them, how should we in the media follow when these stories inevitably arise?

At a minimum, we should make it clear that an old rule now presumed dead—that a politician's private life ought to remain private unless it affects public performance—is worth reviving. It should be the first premise from which news judgments are made. The alternative—to start from the premise that because the technology is so intrusive, because the supermarkets are so full of tabloids, and because some local nightly news team is going to broadcast the story anyway, everything goes—-is to give in to the basest instincts of the culture. So, yes, there is a privacy zone, and, yes, a candidate's sex life is presumed to fall within that zone. But, yes, there will always be legitimate reasons to invade the zone. Reporting about the health and wealth of candidates, for example, is almost always fair game, for self-evident reasons. Private behaviors of any kind that seem, by commonsense standards, to be reckless or over the edge would also seem to be of legitimate public interest.

Obviously, lots of different judgments will be made about what's over the edge. The point is not to have a fixed line, for none can exist, but to have journalists of good will grappling with the need to have a rationale before they cross into the privacy zone. When it comes to sexual behavior, this requirement might wind up making a useful distinction between one candidate who is wantonly promiscuous and another who is quietly adulterous. If this is a distinction that winks at a certain amount of hypocrisy, so be it; some hypocrisy is a helpful lubricant for any well-mannered society. *Washington Post* columnist Charles Krauthammer has advanced a "current and compulsive" standard as a guide on such matters—if a candidate smoked dope or chased women twenty years ago, that's one thing; if he did so to excess, that's another; if he's still doing it, that's still another.[22] The *New York Times* will make different judgments on occasion from CBS or the *Washington Post*, but in the aggregate, a reasonable, commonsense standard that's in sync with mainstream cultural norms is bound to prevail.

But what about the nonelite media? What about the New News? What's the point of the Old News making carefully calibrated news judgments if the information is going to slither into the public square anyway, via the tabloids? One vivid case study is already before us: the Gennifer Flowers story. During the early months of his campaign, the elite media had written stories about Bill Clinton that mentioned he was "dogged by rumors of womanizing." (This was the same formulation the media used in the early weeks of the Hart candidacy in 1987, and it was irresponsible both times. Either such rumors are deemed newsworthy, in which case they should be reported only if verified; or they're deemed not newsworthy, in which case reporting their existence is nothing more than rumor-mongering.) Clinton tried to take the edge off these wink-wink stories by telling reporters that he and his wife had marital difficulties in the past, that things were patched up now, and that he would not discuss any details of his extramarital life. It seemed like a grown-up way to proceed.

Then along came Flowers, with her kiss-and-tell interview in the *Star*, her Manhattan press conference, and her "love tapes" (actually, they were pretty tame) of phone conversations with Clinton. Initially, most newspapers buried the story inside, and ABC and CBS network news programs stayed away from it altogether while NBC lightly touched on the allegations. Many local news programs, however, headlined the story and later that night, ABC News's "Nightline" devoted an entire show to it. Ted Koppel, proclaiming "those of us in . . . the more respectable and reliable news organizations—unless we can confirm that sort of story on our own . . . tend to ignore it," went on, with the help of journalists and others, to worry over the media's coverage of Flowers's interview. Jonathan Alter of *Newsweek*, described the dilemma this way: "You know, it was one of those radioactive stories that I don't think anybody really wanted to deal with. But to mix a metaphor, it's like a big elephant sitting in the living room and when the entire campaign comes to a screeching halt over an issue like this, it's hard to avoid completely. The challenge becomes to put it in context . . . . " Mandy Grunwald, a political consultant, suggested that the format of the Koppel show that evening and other "media" stories was just a way that journalists could "get at the story" without having to check the facts. Koppel looked pained and Alter shrugged agreement, noting that he and others "essentially get the details through customs as a media story. It is a media story, but we are also a little bit hypocritical in not admitting that we are, in fact, spreading it even when we discredit it."[23]

After Koppel's dissection, Clinton—ignoring his own pledge not to discuss the details of such allegations—agreed to appear on CBS's "60 Minutes" for the express purpose of denying Flowers's charges before a huge nationwide audience, and the story became impossible for the Old News to ignore. By my lights, this was a case of a politician intruding on his own zone of privacy (although, to be sure, he was in a damned-if-he-did, damned-if-he-didn't situation). Had he stuck with his original policy of no comment, my guess is that the Flowers story would have still had a run, but it would have been shorter and less sensational. As it turned out, the story got the feeding-frenzy treatment, prompting a great deal of hand-wringing about the sinking of media standards. "It's a terrible thing that the standards of the press are being set by a supermarket tabloid," Stephen Hess of the Brookings Institution said the week after Flowers held her press conference. "And then the others think they can pick up the story and keep their halo polished. Well, they're out of the same ilk, and they're just arguing about price."

Christopher Lydon, a news anchor at Boston's public broadcast station, WGBH, and a former political correspondent for the *New York Times*, made a shrewd observation about the way the Old News and the New News had fed off one another in the Clinton–Flowers case:

> See the pattern? The upscale media baited the trap with hints about womanizing; their downmarket cousins bagged the trophy; and the quality commentators returned, bright clothespins on their noses, to dissect the evidence and tell us what it meant. To audiences it did not look like real warfare in the media but rather like a face-saving division of labor.[24]

"We are sort of becoming the serial killers of democracy," *Boston Globe* columnist Thomas Oliphant said at a media symposium at the University of Minnesota a few weeks after the Flowers story broke. In the old days

> it was unthinkable that something published in a tabloid could be lifted whole, undissected, simply transmitted into what we like to think is the mainstream quality press. But this has now metastasized like a cancer. Reporters and editors who have no self-control are simply acting as a transmission belt for gossip and scandal.[25]

My own sense is that the anguish over this case was overdone, and that members of the media were giving their craft a bit of a bum rap. Sleazy as the story was, if a woman comes forward with a sensational but plausible allegation about a presidential candidate, and the candidate goes to the trouble of seeking a national audience so he can deny it, then it's news, by all the definitions of news that I know about. The question is, how to handle the news. On the whole, I think the Old News did okay, under the circumstances. Some newspapers such as the *New York Times* tried—to their credit—burying the Flowers story deep inside for several days, but gave up when Clinton's nationally televised denial gave the story more thrust. Many tried confirming or refuting the story and discovered—as is so often the case with allegations involving sex—it was virtually impossible to conclusively prove or disprove. While local stations flocked after Flowers, the major network news programs never gave her the exposure of an interview, properly maintaining that she had compromised her credibility by selling her allegations for profit.

It is probably too much to expect that when a juicy—and, this is a key point, seemingly credible—morsel of gossip gets smuggled into the journalistic food chain by the tabloids, the Old News won't take a bite. The question is how big a bite, how long a bite. It's best to follow the European model in these matters—the stories should be briskly exposed, enjoyed, and ignored. The public is perfectly capable of extracting whatever information it chooses to extract from them, then moving along to other matters. Here is where the Old News can be faulted on the Flowers story, but it's more of a quibble than an indictment. For competitive reasons, the media have a habit of dwelling on these stories too long, to the point where their feeding frenzies become "self-referential," to use a nice phrase of the *Washington Post*'s Amy E. Schwartz. She noted that after the Flowers story broke, journalists spent days and days asking Clinton how serious he thought the damage was to his candidacy. "All it means," Schwartz wrote, "is 'Do you think we'll stop asking you this question, governor? Do you think you are going to be able to make us stop asking it?'" She concluded her op-ed piece: "Are we survivable? We and Clinton are about to find out. If we stop, 'it' will stop. If we don't, it won't. It is frightening and disorienting to watch hundreds of colleagues hurl themselves off a cliff in slow motion, all the while wondering out loud whether they can be stopped."[26] Postscript: We stopped. It stopped. Clinton won the nomination. All of which makes the useful point that voters are both fair-minded and forgiving, and perfectly capable, once the din dies down, of keeping things in perspective. After the Hart episode in 1987, some in the media reached the wrongheaded conclusion that adultery had become a disqualifying sin for anyone who would be president. It's never been in the past, it wasn't in 1988, and it isn't today—and we probably have Gennifer Flowers to thank for setting the record straight. To be sure, the issue may yet come back to haunt Clinton again this fall, but this time the voters will have a broader range of character lessons to draw from it—maybe he's an adulterer, and maybe he lied about his adultery, but at least he's not a quitter.

Suppose the juicy tidbits of gossip printed in the tabloids don't have the ring of truth, or suppose they're about behavior that qualifies as private under the fuzzy ground rules outlined above. Then the Old News ought to decline a bite. For it *is* possible for standards to flow from top to bottom. The Old News still has the power to determine whether a sensational story from the New News gets traction or not in the mainstream culture. The relevant example here unfolded in the 1988 campaign, when an alternative newspaper, the *LA Weekly*, printed a long cover story about an alleged extramarital affair that then-Vice President Bush had. The story was totally uncorroborated and—unlike the case with Flowers— the woman in question was never quoted. The elite media, belying their sensationalist reputation, collectively held their breath and ignored the story.[27] It died a quick and deserved death—only to reemerge four years later the week before the 1992 Republican convention. This time the peg was a footnote in a just-published book that quoted a former U.S. diplomat, now dead, claiming that in 1984 he had arranged for then–Vice President Bush and a female member of Bush's staff to stay in adjoining rooms while on an official visit to Geneva. The reference led CNN and NBC correspondents to ask Bush about the long-rumored affair, first in a press conference, later in a taped interview. Both times Bush reacted angrily, denying the charge and scolding the press for bringing it up. His indignation appeared to win him sympathy from the public, and the story once again disappeared after a short run.

Some have inferred from the media's different treatment of Bush and Clinton a double standard—one for Democrats, one for Republicans. It's probably closer to the truth that Democrats seem to have a harder time than Republicans abiding by novelist Nelson Algren's three rules of life: "Never eat at a place called Mom's. Never play cards with a man named Doc. And never have an affair with someone who has more problems than you do."[28] Whatever the case, the facts and the context of the Clinton and Bush stories were quite different, and the responsible media did what the responsible media are supposed to do— they exercised judgment.

Happily, the media's role as the character cops on the campaign trail doesn't always take them into the bedroom. In 1992, two fresh faces bounded onto the national stage—Clinton and Perot. Using biography as the fundamental source, the media did a credible job of digging into their records and reporting stories that helped the public understand who these men are. What did Clinton's cozy relationship with the chicken industry in his state tell us about how he balances his concern for jobs with his concern for the environment? What did Perot's alleged unauthorized blowing up of a coral reef to make way for his boats to dock at his vacation home in Bermuda tell us about his respect for laws and rules? If you were interested, you could learn all about the characters of the men who would be president from the media, and draw your own conclusions. To their credit, the media have been serving up more of this kind of in-depth reporting with each new campaign. Part of this involves digging into a candidate's past, but part can be simply reporting the way the candidate handles the ordeal of running for president. In 1987, political biographer Doris Kearns Goodwin suggested a checklist of questions for political reporters to bring out on the trail with them:

- ▲ How much physical energy does the candidate display? Does he keep humming, or does he run out of gas?
- ▲ How does he react to the experience of the campaign? What does he say he's learned from being out there? How, if at all, has he changed in the reporter's eyes?
- ▲ How is he with people? Does he reach out and touch, or does he seem to shrink from personal and physical contact?
- ▲ How does he deal with, and relate to, his staff? Is he a disciplinarian, a delegator? Does he play them off against each other? And who are they?
- ▲ What does the standard stump speech—and the changes and evolutions in it—tell us about the candidate? There's a reason he gives the speech over and over. What is it?
- ▲ Does he evoke emotion in his crowds? A leader is always in a relationship with his constituency. What relationship does he seek? What does he achieve?
- ▲ Does he have interests beyond politics? When he's not campaigning, can he talk about anything else?
- ▲ Does he have a sense of humor? Of irony? Of detachment? Is his humor always aimed at others, or can he kid himself?
- ▲ What kind of relationship does he have with his political peers? How open is he with them? How candid can they be with him? Who are they?
- ▲ How does he deal with setbacks, aggravations, frustrations? Can he bounce back? Does he scapegoat, shift blame? Is he overwhelmed with guilt?
- ▲ How truthful is his picture of reality? When recounting stories, is he accurate, or does he embroider or shade reality?[29]

Some of this checklist calls for simple observation, some for analysis and interpretation. More and more, with the emergence of New News forms, with the "everywhere culture" putting out so much information to the masses, it's the job of the elite media to provide interpretation, context, analysis. This may seem inconsistent with my earlier recommendation that the elite media back out of the frame every now and then so the candidates and voters can have more unmediated conversation with one another. In fact, both roles are essential; the Old News must be both a transmission belt and an analyst of what's been transmitted. It must legitimate some of the babble that's pumped into the culture twenty-four hours a day, ignore some of the babble, shoot down some of the babble. For better or worse, it has to be both player and referee. But when it is in its mode of analyst, it must strive for balance. The search for warts cannot be more important than the recognition of virtues. Most journalists I know—myself included—need to overcome their fear of flacking, that panicky feeling that if you write something admiring of a politician, he just might abscond with the widow's and orphan's fund next Tuesday. And then who looks like a fool?

There was a time when journalists were too deferential to authority; for the past generation or so, we have been too hostile. We have been lead players in a culture of disparagement, an adversary culture. Worse, we have managed in recent years to miss the truly big scandals in government and politics—the savings and loan fiasco, for example—while we play to populist anger by dwelling too long on small warts, petty thievery, and easy exposés.

Americans have always harbored a populist distrust of the ruling class—it's what gave birth to the idea of America. Our greatest humorist, Mark Twain, called politicians "the only distinctly native criminal class." Some of this distrust is healthy, but taken too far, it becomes destructive. "A culture whose elites trash its institutions, its elected officials and its instruments of government is a culture that courts a world best explained by Hobbes," says University of California at Berkeley political scientist Nelson W. Polsby. We in the elite media have been trashing too much too long and too loosely. It's time for balance. Social commentator Irving Kristol got it right two decades ago:

> The older populist journalism was always ready, when things went wrong, to shout: "Shoot the piano player!" The new demagogic journalism is constantly and no less shrilly suggesting: "Shoot the piano." I fear that this sort of thing can be contagious. Before we know it someone will be shooting up

the whole saloon and, in the process, destroying some irre-
placeable spirits.[30]

   The changes suggested above must come from within the hearts,
souls, and minds of journalists. Are there other fixes that can be
imposed from without? I think so. Some useful changes have already
been foisted on the Old News by the New, especially bringing the voter
back into the conversation with long-format interviews and call-in shows.
But there are limits to this good; it is better contained on the campaign
trail than brought into the halls of government. The drafters of our
Constitution chose a representative democracy rather than a direct
democracy because they understood that public passions needed to
be filtered before being translated into national action. Within a
decade, perhaps sooner, the technology will exist to conduct electronic
national town halls, at which citizens can sit in their own living
rooms, watch their leaders debate matters of national concern on television, then press one button to declare war or another to cut taxes.
There are real dangers here. "The electronic town hall, like other
trappings of techno-democracy, is an illusion," writes columnist
Charles Krauthammer:

> In a vast continental nation like the United States . . . mass elec-
> tronic communication is really one-way communication,
> top-down. For the practiced performer the call-in show is the
> most easily manipulated forum, [which is why] every two-bit
> Mussolini adopts it as his own. Pomp and plebiscites. The Duce
> and his people. No need for the messy stuff in between. Not
> for nothing did the founders abhor direct democracy. They
> knew it to be a highway to tyranny.[31]

Harvard professor of government Harvey Mansfield made the same
point in an article in *The New Republic* in early July, shortly before Perot
dropped out:

> [Perot] is taking advantage of our failure to understand the need
> for space between government and people in a democracy.
> Constitutional space allows the government to do its job
> without having to fear unpopularity, and it enables the peo-
> ple to stand back from the government and judge what it has
> done without too much prejudicial involvement. For how
> could a people blame a government that has acted in accor-
> dance with the buttons the people themselves had pushed?[32]

While the media are on the right track in permitting more citizens to communicate with candidates during the *campaign,* their more pressing challenge is to do a better job of allowing the candidates to communicate with the voters. Once, political parties served as the vital communication link from politicians to voters. This was the era of the clubhouse meeting and the torchlight parade, the era (in the mid- to late nineteenth century) when turnouts hovered around 80 percent in presidential campaigns. People cared deeply about politics—it was a way to participate in the life of the community and nation before television and radio dampened appetites for such communal pastimes. The labels "Democrat" and "Republican" gave voters a sense of belonging, and issues a sense of coherence. The parties served to frame public affairs around a stable cluster of principles and policies. Today's vestigial parties have lost their ability to articulate or defend political ideas, and it's been a generation since they've given anyone but a band of operatives and ideologues the feeling that they belong to something larger than themselves. Television has supplanted them; nowadays, a political rally is three people in front of a television screen. But in drawing politics into the voters' living rooms, television has driven it out of their orbit of interest. The image of politics television presents is a montage of manipulative candidates, cynical reporters, distorted attack ads, and demagogic appeals. There aren't many sympathetic figures in this picture, nor is there much room for a nourishing dialogue.

The challenge now is to turn television into an ally of reasoned political debate, not an enemy. We need to create a new forum on television that would compete with the thirty-second spots and the eight-second sound bites, but in a format partial to words over images, reason over fakery, substance over trivia. It may seem paradoxical to try to revive the political discourse by forcing more of it onto a medium that contributes so mightily to its anemia. But any serious reform has to go straight to the belly of the beast, for that's where the conversation "happens" for the great majority of Americans.

Here's one idea: a five-minute fix. Each candidate for president should be given five minutes of free time a night, on alternating nights, simultaneously on every television and radio station in the country for the final five weeks of the presidential campaign. If this plan were to go in effect this fall, George Bush would have five minutes on Monday, September 28 at, say 8:55 p.m. on the nation's roughly fifteen hundred television stations and eleven thousand radio stations. Clinton would have the same five minute slot on Tuesday, Bush Wednesday, Clinton Thursday, and so on.

In return for the grant of free time, each candidate would agree to one simple format restriction: he (or his running mate) would have to appear on the air for the entire five minutes. No surrogates. No journalists. No opponents. No Willie Horton. Just the candidate, making his best case to a somewhat captive audience of roughly sixty million a night, five minutes at a pop.

Is there any guarantee this would elevate the conversation? Actually, no. Nothing in this format would prevent a candidate from blathering on about "climbing every mountain," or from launching a load of mud at his opponent if he were convinced that either of these appeals would win him votes. But there are, embedded in this proposal, a number of disincentives to engage in that kind of discourse. First, there is the check of personal accountability. If a candidate chose to devote his five minutes to mindless happy talk or slanderous attack, at least he would have to put his face and voice on the line; no more crafty political consultants doing the dirty work while the candidate's fingers stay clean—at least for that night. Next, there is the certainty of swift response. What one candidate says one night, his opponent can refute or counterattack the next—same time, same stations, same massive audience, an even playing field. Finally, there is the prohibition against images. Although the attacker can distort with words as well as pictures, the target always has a better chance to defend against words. Visual attacks operate in the realm of emotion, not reason. (In 1988, once the menacing face of Willie Horton was shown on television again and again—many more viewers saw it, by the way, in news reports than in paid ads—it became difficult to hold a rational conversation about crime and punishment.) Visual attacks are often unanswerable by linguistic debate, which is why, increasingly in political campaigns, they provoke not a defense but an equally emotion-laden visual counterattack. Verbal assaults, on the other hand, can be parsed, dissected, rebutted, and refuted. In this sense even a sharply distorted verbal attack is more conducive to reasoned debate that a subtly manipulative image. When it comes to political discourse, the old adage needs to be turned upside down: A word is worth a thousand pictures.

Suppose we were to achieve this goal of a more elevated campaign debate for five minutes a night. So what? Wouldn't it still be drowned out by the more visually stimulating thirty-second attack ads, or the more pervasive cynicism of the broadcast journalists? Perhaps. But there are three elements of this free time plan that would allow it to hold its own against the babble: simultaneity, brevity, and repetition.

Of the three, simultaneity is by far the most important. The idea that nearly everyone in America who has a radio or television on at 8:55

p.m. in the last month of a campaign has to see and hear the same message would, in and of itself, concentrate attention. Millions would no doubt resent this forced feeding of politics. These viewers could escape to cable channels (they are not subject to the same public interest standard that broadcasters are, and therefore it is doubtful they could be compelled to give the free time) or to a movie on their videocassette recorders, or to the bathroom. So be it; these are safety valves to coerced viewing. As for the opposite concern, that remote control zappers and other switch-off options make the electronic roadblock too porous, it's hard to see a cause for complaint. People have walked out on speeches since the first politician took the podium. No channel of communication can capture everyone, no matter how ruthlessly designed. What matters is not that millions of viewer would escape, but that tens of millions wouldn't.

If you are going to pass a law that tries to force political dialogue on viewers this way, you owe it to them to make that dialogue as palatable as possible. This is where brevity comes into play. The free-time proposals that have been advocated in this country over the years (including a 1969 Twentieth Century Fund proposal put forward by former Federal Communications Commission chairman Newton Minow), as well as some of those in place in Western Europe and elsewhere, provide for time in fifteen- or thirty-minute segments. This is too long, for it guarantees that the viewership would be small and that the politicians would be preaching to the converted—to that segment of the public that already is tuned in to public life. The same flaw bedevils two other otherwise laudable proposals put forward in recent years: one from the Harvard Kennedy School's Shorenstein Barone Center, calling for nine Sunday evenings of ninety minutes of television programming on issues and candidate debate, to rotate among the networks throughout the fall presidential campaign; another from University of Texas at Austin Government Department chairman James S. Fishkin, calling for a televised national issues convention at which candidates would answer questions from a random panel of citizens, who would then vote on which one did best.[33]

The crying need in our massively depoliticized society today is not to create ingenious new offerings for that slice of the viewing public that already has available to it more information than it can possibly digest from MacNeil/Lehrer, C-SPAN, and CNN, from Dan, Peter and Tom, and so on. The need is to reach the inattentive audience; the ninety-one million adult Americans who didn't bother to vote for president in 1988, the tens of millions of others who think politics is baloney. Five minutes is long enough to say something substantive to these apolitical television watchers, but brief enough to keep most of them parked on their couches while they wait for Homer Simpson or Roseanne to help them forget their worries. The longer the format, the more brutal the falloff in viewership—and therefore, the fewer segments that could be made available to the public. The traffic simply won't bear a half hour of political speechmaking night after night in prime time; witness the long-term drop-off in viewership of the political conventions. This trade-off—longer speeches but fewer of them—is a lousy deal. Repetition is a powerful agent of marketing.

Ideally, these five-minute presentations, repeated night after night, would unfold as a serialized debate, with thrust and parry, charge and rebuttal, gambits and surprises—in short, the very attributes of drama that journalism's master narrative is always looking to superimpose onto campaigns anyway. But these exchanges would have a fighting chance to be substantive. "You'd almost be forced to really get into the issues," the late Lee Atwater, former chairman of the Republican National Committee and architect of President Bush's hollow flag-and-furlough campaign in 1988, said of this proposed five-minute fix, "because if the American people knew the five minutes had been set aside every night for political debate, they'd want something substantive put before them. A candidate who tried to get away with junk would get eaten up." Moreover, if the presentations were substantive, they—and not the photo ops or the thirty-second spots—would be replayed and amplified on the network news shows and in the morning headlines. They might even be what voters talked about at the grocery checkout line and the office watercooler. Over time, a dialogue of this nature might even breed a new respect for politics—and thereby diminish the payoff for ads that traffic in distortion and demagoguery, and for journalism that plays to cynicism and populist anger. In other words, by reversing the spiral of diminishing expectations, the five-minute fix might elevate the political discourse across the board.

If it proves successful in the presidential campaign, free time ought to be expanded to cover races for all levels of government. The problem is to figure out how a single, short segment format could accommodate the thousands of federal, state, and local races held every even-numbered year. To take the most challenging example, New York City's media market alone encompasses three states, nearly forty congressional districts, and hundreds of state legislative districts. The solution is surprisingly simple. Don't guarantee five minutes to every candidate for every office. Simply allot five minutes of "local time" to every state party on alternating nights (one night Democrats, one night Republicans, one night independent third parties that meet thresholds of viability) in the final five weeks of every campaign year, and let them figure out which of their candidates gets to use what portion of the five minutes in each media market of the state. If the state party leaders behave in their self-interest, the most competitive races would get the most exposure—good for challengers, good for voters, good for democracy, and good for the political parties. There's a kind of poetic justice hereby allocating free time to political parties, we would be turning the agent of their demise, television, into the theater of their revival. Nothing is more valuable to a political candidate—especially an underfunded challenger—than free media exposure. If parties could decide who got these freebies and who didn't, they would have something of considerable value to dispense. They could reward and they could punish, and this new power could produce at least a small turn back away from the atomized, every-man-for-himself brand of politics and government that has made Congress such an unwieldy institution in the past generation.

If free time is such a good idea, why hasn't anybody thought of it before? As a matter of fact, lots of people have thought of it before. More than half a century ago, Frank Knox, the 1936 GOP nominee for vice president, proposed in a speech: "Why not . . . require that, near election time, both great political parties be allowed, without expense, an equal amount of time on the air, to the end that both sides of all issues be fairly and adequately presented to the people." Nine years later, just such a proposal was adopted nationwide. The nation, however, was Great Britain. It instituted "party political broadcasts" (PPBs) on radio in 1945 and television in 1951. During national campaigns in England, which are mercifully brief, the two leading parties are given blocks of time to make their appeals (lesser parties are given shorter blocks, in proportion to their number of seats in Parliament). No paid commercials are allowed on British television. This broadcast model for handling campaigns on television has been adopted, in whole or part, by nearly all of the world's industrialized democracies. But it has never taken root here—in part because we have a weak party system, in part because our advertising/marketing culture is so powerful, and in part because the idea of regulating political speech in any way, shape, or format cuts against the grain. There have been several serious free-time proposals in this country over the years, however—from Minow's 1969 report for the Twentieth Century Fund to a Senate campaign finance reform bill introduced in 1991 that would offer chits for television time to candidates who agreed to limit their campaign spending.

The proposals never go anywhere in Congress because they offend two critical interest groups—the broadcast industry, which instinctively recoils from any legislation that would intrude on its hegemony over its own programming, and incumbent members of Congress, who worry that free time would be a boon to challengers. As for the second objection, there have been four consecutive congressional campaigns (1984, 1986, 1988, and 1990) in which 95 percent or more of all incumbent House members standing for reelection have won reelection—a record of noncompetitiveness unprecedented in modern American political history.[34] During this same stretch, approval ratings for Congress have been horrendously low, suggesting that what's going on here isn't approbation; it's ossification. People are so fed up with politics that they have dropped out, given up, and let incumbents rig the election game in their favor—witness the ten-, fifteen-, and twenty-to-one bulges in contributions from political action committees that incumbents enjoy over challengers. One ham-handed way to make congressional campaigns more competitive is to limit terms—forcing the worthy legislators out to pasture with the cads, just for the sin of having hung around too long. The more intelligent way is with free television time, which levels the playing field between incumbents and challengers.

As for the broadcast industry's understandable concern about regulation, any print journalist has to tread diplomatically over this turf. But the legal reality is that newspapers enjoy the full protection of the First Amendment and therefore cannot be regulated, while the broadcast industry enjoys only limited protection. The Radio Act of 1927 and the Communications Act of 1934 established that the airwaves were a federal resource—like a national park—and determined that the exclusive use of this resource be granted to licensees who pledged to uphold "the public interest." In return for this promise, licensees would be given local monopolies over a frequency, free of charge, and a guarantee that the government would not censor broadcast signals. Thus, broadcasters have always had a hybrid status, possessing private rights as well as a public trusteeship. To help ensure that they meet their public trust, Congress and the FCC have over the years established such standards as the equal opportunity rule, reasonable access, and the Fairness Doctrine. Broadcasters have long chafed at these rules, but their key constitutional challenges have always failed. In short, Congress could pass a law tomorrow requiring that all broadcasters provide blocks of free time to political candidates and parties.

But Congress isn't so inclined. Frustrated by years of inaction, former FCC general counsel Henry Geller, a longtime crusader for raising the level of political discourse on television, has been trying for the past year to persuade the three major network executives to *voluntarily* give up three or five minutes a night of free time in the final month of the 1992 presidential campaign. Although he got a good hearing from the networks, especially from ABC, the idea never flew. "One of the problems was that with all of the new attention being paid to politics on television in the spring, the networks took the position, 'Why is this trip necessary?'" Geller said in the summer of 1992. "The answer, of course, is that the people who are watching these long interviews are the people who are already interested in politics. The ones you most want to reach are the ones you can only get by inserting these segments right in the middle of the prime time schedule."

This goes to the heart of what makes the proposal difficult to swallow—it smacks of big-brotherism in a society where people cherish the freedom to do exactly what they want, exactly when they want. And these days, the Perot bubble notwithstanding, they don't want to have much to do with politics.

No matter how much critics deplore the sketchiness of television's political coverage, political scientist Austin Ranney observed almost a decade ago in his book *Channels of Power,* "it is possible that television news puts out considerably more political information than most Americans really want . . . . "[35] In the same vein, sociologist Michael Schudson has written: "In a sense, journalists are the patrons of political life . . . the journalism of the national newsweeklies, most large metropolitan newspapers and the network television news does not mirror the world but constructs one in which the political realm is pre-eminent."[36]

It's no easy thing to graft an interest in politics onto an apolitical citizenry—no matter whether the disinterest stems from populist anger, as it seems to now, or happy apathy, as it has in the past. But the best way to encourage better citizenship is to give citizens better political discourse. H. G. Wells once described campaigns as the feast of democracy. For too long in our country they have been junk food—a steady diet of attack ads, sound bites, photo ops, feeding frenzies. Small wonder that voter turnout in 1988 fell to 50.2 percent—its lowest level in this country in sixty-four years, and roughly twenty-five percentage points lower than the rest of the world's advanced democracies. Presidential campaigns are the one moment every four years when every citizen in America, even the most disconnected, tunes in to the dialogue of democracy, at least for a little while. As long as we have their attention, let's give them a better meal. The moment is too precious to squander.

Notes

1. "The 1992 Campaign: Turnout in Democratic Primaries Hits New Low," *New York Times*, July 2, 1992, p. A14.

2. Jon Katz, "Rock, Rap and Movies Bring You the News," *Rolling Stone*, March 5, 1992, p. 35.

3. Carl Bernstein, "The Idiot Culture," *The New Republic*, June 8, 1992, pp. 24–25.

4. Kiku Adatto, "Sound Bite Democracy: Network Evening News Presidential Campaign Coverage, 1968 and 1988," research paper R-2, June 1990, Joan Shorenstein Barone Center on Press, Politics and Public Policy, Harvard University, p. 23.

5. Daniel C. Hallin, "Sound Bite Democracy," *Wilson Quarterly*, Spring 1992, p. 34.

6. This and all other unattributed quotations are from interviews conducted by the author during Spring and Summer 1992.

7. Nicholas Lemann, "Survival of the Loudest," *New York Times*, July 12, 1992, sec. 4, p. 21.

8. Gwen Ifill, "For Clinton, Attention Grows, Problems Remain," *New York Times*, June 21, 1992, sec. 4, p. 1.

9. Michael Kinsley, "Ask a Silly Question," *The New Republic*, July 6, 1992, p. 6.

10. Jon Katz, "The Media's Myth of the Bloody Campaign," *Rolling Stone*, April 16, 1992, p. 32.

11. Hallin, "Sound Bite Democracy," p. 37.

12. Poll conducted by the Gordon S. Black Corporation, Rochester, New York, released June 3, 1992.

13. Michael Cornfield, "How to Read the Campaign," *Wilson Quarterly*, Spring 1992, p. 46.

14. Hallin, "Sound Bite Democracy," p. 37.

15. Louis Menand, "A Farewell to the '80s," *The New Republic*, October 9, 1989.

16. Jay Rosen, "No Content: The Press, Politics, and Public Philosophy," *Tikkun*, May/June 1992, p. 14.

17. Ibid., p. 78.

18. Peter Trueman, "Don't Stop Talking Mr. Candidate, Your Time Isn't Up," *Toronto Star*, July 31, 1992, p. SW72.

19. Michael K. Frisby, "Crunch Time in the Empire State," *Boston Globe*, March 28, 1992, p. 1.

20. Joseph Pulitzer, "The College of Journalism," *North America Review*, May 1904.

21. I'm the reporter who asked Gary Hart whether he had ever committed adultery. I put the question to him at the press conference three days after the *Miami Herald* story appeared, after Hart had denied doing anything immoral with Donna Rice and claimed he had always held himself to the highest standards of personal conduct. I thought then—and still think today—that his line of defense

invited journalistic inquiry into what those standards were and whether he had ever breached them in the past. But I also thought then—and still think today—that reporters shouldn't go posing the "Big A" question to everyone who runs for president. Hart brought the question on himself, first by his behavior, then by his denial. If you're a frontrunning presidential candidate who chooses to take an overnight voyage to Bimini, on a boat named Monkey Business, with a woman who is half your age and not your wife, you're asking to be asked.

22.   Charles Krauthammer, "The Press Confronts Its Power," *Washington Post*, January 31, 1992, p. A19.

23.   All quotations are from the transcript of "Nightline," January 23, 1992, "Tabloid Prints New Bill Clinton Infidelity Allegations" (Denver: Journal Graphics, 1992).

24.   Christopher Lydon, "Sex, War and Death: Covering Clinton Became a Test of Character—for the Press," *Columbia Journalism Review*, May/June 1992, p. 58.

25.   From "Politics and the Media: Improving the Public Dialogue," conference report on the Mondale Policy Forum, Hubert H. Humphrey Institute of Public Affairs, University of Minnesota, February 6–7, 1992.

26.   Amy E. Schwartz, "Endless Questions," *Washington Post*, January 29, 1992, p. A21.

27.   In October 1988, whether or not to print the story became more complicated when the stock market fell forty points on the false rumor that the *Washington Post* was going to print a story on George Bush's alleged affair. The press was confronted with having to report a real event in the world—the stock market down forty points in one hour—without explaining exactly what the rumor was. Everyone handled it gingerly by saying the stock market fell on a false rumor that the *Post* was about to publish something about Bush's private life.

28.   Nelson Algren, as paraphrased by Jim Hoagland in the *Washington Post*, January 31, 1992, p. A19.

29.   From an internal memorandum circulated at the *Washington Post.*

30.   Irving Kristol, *Crisis for Journalism: The Missing Elite, Press, Politics and Popular Government Domestic Affairs Studies* (Washington, D.C.: American Enterprise Institute, 1972), p. 52.

31.   Charles Krauthammer, "Ross Perot and the Call-In Presidency," *Time*, July 13, 1992, p. 84.

32.   Harvey Mansfield, "Only Amend," *The New Republic*, July 6, 1992, p. 13.

33.   James S. Fishkin's proposal, first raised in his book *Democracy and Deliberation: New Directions for Democratic Reform* (New Haven, Conn.: Yale University Press, 1992), will be aired this fall by WETA-TV.

34.   In fact, according to Ray Smock, House historian, in 1800, 95 percent of all House incumbents who ran for reelection were reelected; in 1802, the figure was 94.6 percent, followed by 98 percent and 97 percent in 1804 and 1806, respectively.

35.   Austin Ranney, *Channels of Power: The Impact of Television on American Politics* (New York: Basic Books, 1983).

36.   Michael Schudson, "The Politics of Narrative Form: The Emergence of News Conventions in Print and Television," *Daedalus*, Fall 1982, p. 107.

Index

ABC, 5, 24

Accountability of public officials, 7

Accuracy in Media (AIM), 9

Adversarial stance, 8

Ad Watch, 47

Agenda for political reporting, 6–7, 8, 11, 25, 28–29

Aggressive style in television journalism, 18, 23–24

Ailes, Roger, 17

Algren, Nelson, 57

Allen, Henry, 22, 24

Allen, John, 13

Alter, Jonathan, 54

Atwater, Lee, 64

Authority of the reporter, 23

Balance of the press, 8

Bernstein, Carl, 40

Bias, media, 8–9

Bill of Rights, 21

Bollinger, Lee C., 19

Bond, Richard, 43–44

Boston Globe, 5, 28, 55

British television, prohibition of paid political ads, 65

Broder, David, 7, 11, 15–16, 31n, 47

Brokaw, Tom, 43

Brookings Institution, 44, 55

Bush, George, 64

Call-in show format, 20

   comparison with professional interviews, 45

Call-in shows, 41

Campaign consultants, 16

Campaign reform

   with free, limited, prime time, 61–65

   to raise the level of political communication, 67

Campaigns versus elections, 48–49

Candidate interviews, New News, 41

Candidates versus the journalists, 44

CBS, 24

Center for Media and Public Affairs (CMPA), 41, 50

Channels of Power (Ranney), 67

Charlotte Observer, 31n

Clinton, Bill, 17, 50, 57–58

   Nielsen ratings, 42–43

Code of standard practices, 39

Collins, Gail, 7, 18

Columbus: Beyond 2000, 12–15

Columbus, Georgia, 11–15

Coming to Public Judgment (Yankelovich), 26–27

Committee on Media Integrity (Comint), 9

Communications Act of 1934, 66

Communication with the voters, 61

Confrontation, aggressive, with politicians, 6

Congressional incumbents, response to free time, 66

Conversation, politics as, 10, 49

Cornfield, Michael, 47

Credibility of journalists, 6–7, 14

Criticism, informed use of, 6

Culture
  adversary, of journalism, 59
  of the newsroom, 4
  political, and media bias, 8–9

Demagoguery, electronic, 7
Democracy
  and the electronic town hall, 60
  and the public's right to discussion
    and debate, 7
DeParle, Jason, 21–22
Detachment, principled, 8
Donahue, Phil, 17, 42

Elections versus campaigns, 48–49
Electoral politics, political reality in,
  10–11, 16
Electronic demagoguery, 7
Electronic fundraising, 41
Elite media, 38–39, 43
Ethical code of journalists, 8

Fairness of the press, 8
Fairness and Accuracy in Reporting
  (FAIR), 9
Federalist No. 84, 21
"feeding frenzy" mentality, 5, 17, 56
First Amendment, significance of, 19
Fishkin, James S., 63
Frankel, Max, 5
Free media time, 61–65

Geller, Henry, 66–67
Gergen, David, 50
Goodwin, Doris Kearns, 58
"gotcha" stories, 6
Government regulation
  and broadcasting's First Amendment
    rights, 66
  and the citizen's right to information,
    19
Grunwald, Mandy, 54

Hallin, Daniel C., 41, 46, 47
Hamilton, Alexander, 21
Handlers, 16

Hart, Gary, 51, 68–69n
Havel, Vaclav, 9
Hess, Stephen, 44, 55

Image, claims of interest groups to
  presentation of, 9
Image advisers, 11
Image politics, 10–11
  elimination of, in free media time,
    62–65
Images of a Free Press (Bollinger), 19
Imus, Don, 42
Information versus quality of public
  opinion, 27
Interest group politics, 10–11
  and free campaign time, 65–66

Jennings, Peter, 5
Johnson, Al, 31n
Journalism
  as an art of public life, 27–28
  checklist of questions for political
    reporters, 58–59
  code of standard practices of, 39
  as a craft, 51, 52
  standards for respect of privacy,
    53–57
Journalists
  as actors in politics, 7, 22, 28–29, 48
  as advocates for public communi
    cation, 24–25
  versus the candidates, 44
  function as observers, 23
  as observers, 8
  philosophy of, 3, 8–9, 24–25
  as political activists, 8, 16, 28–29
  views of press performance, 5–6
Judgment of responsible media, 57
Just, Ward, 5

Katz, Jon, 4, 46
Kennedy, John F., 52
King, Larry, 45
Kinsley, Michael, 45
Know-Everythingism and Know-
  Nothingism, 51–52

Knox, Frank, 65
Koppel, Ted, 54
Krauthammer, Charles, 53, 60
Kristol, Irving, 59–60

Lasch, Christopher, 27–28, 48–49
LA Weekly, 57
Ledger-Enquirer (Columbus, Georgia), 28, 11–15
Lemann, Nicholas, 41–42
Leno, Jay, 43
Lewis, Anthony, 5
Lichter, S. Robert, 41, 44
Lydon, Christopher, 55

Mansfield, Harvey, 60–61
Media, 4
    bias in, 8–9
    elite, 38–39
    nonelite, 54–57
    views of owners' of, 31
Menand, Louis, 47–48
Merritt, Davis, Jr., 31n
Metaphor of conversation, 10
Miami Herald, 51
Minow, Newton, 63
Murrow, Edward R., 24

NBC, 5
Neutrality, polling as a means to, 26
New Media Order, 37–38
New News, 38
    lessons for the Old, 60
    standards of, 40
New Republic, The, 40, 45, 47–48, 60–61
Newsday, 7
Newsweek, 54
New York Times, 3, 5, 22, 56
New York Times v. Sullivan (1964), 18
Nielsen ratings, 42–43

Objectivity of the press, 8
Observers, journalists as, 8
Old News
    definition of, 39
    public discontent with, 46

Oliphant, Thomas, 5, 55
Opinion polling, 25–27
    for reaching a verdict, 26
Oppositional stance, 16–17

Perot, H. Ross, 41, 57–58
    Nielsen ratings on "Today," 42
Persian Gulf War, reporting during, 21–22
Political parties, revival of, 65–66
Political reality, 10–11
    agenda for reporting on, 15–16
    questions for reporting on, 59
Political vision
    as a disciplining force, 6
    of the process of self-government, 9–10
Politics
    decay of, 29n
    the process of self-government, 7
    reconnection with government, 7
    state of American, 3
    views of political reality, 10–11
    agenda for, 28
Polsby, Nelson W., 59
Popular culture, reflection of middle-class populism in, 38–39
Poynter Institute for Media Studies, 31n
Presidential campaign
    five-point agenda for reporting on, 15–16
    of 1988, 4–5
    of 1992, 5
    Old News presentation versus New News, 40
    proposed free television time for, 61–65
    reform of coverage of, 46–47
Press
    definitions of, 4
    as a political instrument, 7–8
Privacy, and public life, 49–50, 52–57
Propaganda, the press as a delivery device for, 6
Public Agenda Foundation, 25

Public debate versus information, 27
Public discourse, raising the level of,
    38–39
Public judgment versus public opin-
    ion, 25–27
Public opinion, quality of, 27
Public politics
    definition of, 10–11
    for determining a city's future, 14–15
Pulitzer, Joseph, 50

Race relations, community actions to
    shape, 13–15
Radio Act of 1927, 66
Ranney, Austin, 67
Red Lion Broadcasting Co. v. FCC
    (1969), 19
Reform of presidential campaign cov-
    erage, 46–47
Rhetoric of political reporting, 8
Right to adequate information, 19
Rolling Stone, 46
Roosevelt, Franklin D., 52
Rosen, Jay, 38–39, 48–49
Roth, Melissa, 17–18
Ryan, Randolph, 28

Sabato, Larry, 5
Sandel, Michael, 10, 49
"Saturday Night Live," 21–22
Schudson, Michael, 67
Schwartz, Amy E., 56
Self-government, journalists' roles in
    promoting, 16
Sevareid, Eric, 24
Smock, Ray, 69n
Sorenson, Erik, 49
Sound bites, length of, 41, 46, 49, 61
"Spin doctors," 11
Standards for reporting on private
    lives, 53–57
State and local campaigns, proposed
    free television time for, 65–66
Stephanopoulous, George, 43
Stock market response to rumor, 69n
Sununu, John, 21–22

Swift, Jack, 13–15, 31n

Talk-Show America, 37
Taylor, Paul, 20
Television
    ambiance of coverage, 42
    British, free television time on, 65
    negative spin of coverage, 50
    replacement of political rallies
        with, 61
Tough reporting
    a constructive philosophy of, 14
    as the default agenda of the press,
        16–17
    as the journalists' reason for being,
        20
    reflection in aggressive television
        interviewing, 18
Truth
    in a free society, 9
    journalists' pursuit of, 24
Twain, Mark, 59
Tyranny, and direct democracy, 60

United Beyond 2000, 13–14
University of California, San
    Diego, 41
U.S. News & World Report, 50

Vanocur, Sander, 5
Verdict of public opinion, 26
Vision of politics, 24–25
Visual versus verbal attacks, 62

Wallace, Chris, 24
Walters, Barbara, 45
Washington Post, 5, 7, 22, 47, 53, 56
"Watchdog" role, 8
Watson, Billy, 14
Wells, H. G., 67
Wichita Eagle, 31n

Yankelovich, Daniel, 25, 26–27

Zero-sum game, interest politics as,
    10–11

About the Authors

Jay Rosen is an associate professor of journalism at New York University, and an associate of the Kettering Foundation. His essays on the media and public life have appeared in *Harper's*, the *Los Angeles Times*, the *Nation*, *Tikkun*, and numerous other journals. He is presently completing a book entitled *What Are Journalists For?*, in which a revised version of this paper will appear.

Paul Taylor is a former politics writer for the *Washington Post* and author of *See How They Run* (Knopf, 1990), a book about media coverage of the 1988 campaign, from which parts of this paper have been adapted. In mid-1992, he became the *Post*'s correspondent in South Africa.